Communications in Computer and Information Science 1462

Rasmus Adler · Amel Bennaceur ·
Simon Burton · Amleto Di Salle · Nicola Nostro ·
Rasmus Løvenstein Olsen · Selma Saidi ·
Philipp Schleiss · Daniel Schneider ·
Hans-Peter Schwefel (Eds.)

Dependable Computing – EDCC 2021 Workshops

DREAMS, DSOGRI, SERENE 2021
Munich, Germany, September 13, 2021
Proceedings

Springer

Editors
Rasmus Adler
Fraunhofer IESE
Kaiserslautern, Germany

Simon Burton
Fraunhofer IKS
Munich, Germany

Nicola Nostro ⓘ
ResilTech S.R.L.
Pontedera, Italy

Selma Saidi
TU Dortmund
Dortmund, Germany

Daniel Schneider
Fraunhofer IESE
Kaiserslautern, Germany

Amel Bennaceur ⓘ
The Open University
Milton Keynes, UK

Amleto Di Salle ⓘ
University of L'Aquila
L'Aquila, Italy

Rasmus Løvenstein Olsen
Aalborg University
Aalborg, Denmark

Philipp Schleiss
Fraunhofer IKS
Munich, Germany

Hans-Peter Schwefel
Aalborg University
Aalborg, Denmark

ISSN 1865-0929   ISSN 1865-0937 (electronic)
Communications in Computer and Information Science
ISBN 978-3-030-86506-1   ISBN 978-3-030-86507-8 (eBook)
https://doi.org/10.1007/978-3-030-86507-8

This Springer imprint is published by the registered company Springer Nature Switzerland AG
The registered company address is: Gewerbestrasse 11, 6330 Cham, Switzerland

Preface

The European Dependable Computing Conference (EDCC) is an international annual forum for researchers and practitioners to present and discuss their latest research results on theory, techniques, systems, and tools for the design, validation, operation, and evaluation of dependable and secure computing systems. Traditionally, one-day workshops precede the main conference: the workshops complement the main conference by addressing dependability or security issues in specific application domains or by focussing on specialized topics, such as system resilience.

The 17th edition of EDCC (EDCC 2021) was initially planned to be held in Munich, Germany, during September 13–16, 2021. Due to the COVID-19 pandemic, for the second year in a row, it was changed to a virtual conference. The workshops day was held on Monday, September 13, 2021. Four workshop proposals were submitted to EDCC 2021, and, after a thoughtful revision process led by the workshop chair, all of them were accepted. The evaluation criteria for the selection process included the relevance to EDCC, the timeliness and expected interest in the proposed topics, the organizers' ability to lead a successful workshop, and their balance and synergy.

These joint proceedings include the accepted papers from the following three workshops:

- Workshop on Dynamic Risk managEment for Autonomous Systems (DREAMS)
- Workshop on Dependable SOlutions for Intelligent Electricity Distribution GRIds (DSOGRI)
- Workshop on Software Engineering for Resilient Systems (SERENE)

The fourth workshop, Critical Automotive Applications: Robustness and Safety (CARS), will not be published as part of the Springer proceedings: the workshops organizers decided to continue the publication strategy they have followed since the first CARS workshop in 2010.

Each workshop had an independent Program Committee, which was in charge of reviewing and selecting the papers submitted to the workshop. All the workshops adopted a single-blind review process and the workshop papers received three reviews per paper on average.

Many people contributed to the success of the EDCC 2021 workshops day. I would like to express my gratitude to all those supported this event. I thank all the workshops organizers for their dedication and commitment, the authors who contributed to this volume, the reviewers for their help in the paper assessment, and the workshops participants.

I would also like to thank all the members of the EDCC Steering and Organizing Committees, in particular Michael Paulitsch and Mario Trapp (the general chairs), who made this virtual edition possible and free of charge for all the participants with the support of Intel Deutschland GmbH and Fraunhofer IKS, and André Martin (the publication chair) for his help in the preparation of these proceedings.

Finally, many thanks to the staff of Springer who provided professional support through all the phases that led to this volume.

September 2021   Ilir Gashi

Organization

EDCC Steering Committee

Karama Kanoun	LAAS-CNRS, France
Felicita Di Giandomenico	CNR-ISTI, Italy
Jean-Charles Fabre	LAAS-CNRS, Toulouse, France
Johan Karlsson	Chalmers University of Technology, Sweden
Henrique Madeira	Universidade de Coimbra, Portugal
Miroslaw Malek	Università della Svizzera Italiana, Switzerland
Michael Paulitsch	Intel, Germany
Alexander Romanovsky	Newcastle University, UK
Juan Carlos Ruiz Technical	University of Valencia, Spain
Janusz Sosnowski	Warsaw University of Technology, Poland

EDCC 2021 Organization

General Chairs

Michael Paulitsch	Intel, Germany
Mario Trapp	Fraunhofer IKS,Germany

Program Chair

Jérémie Guiochet	LAAS-CNRS, France

Web Chairs

William Andersen	Intel, Germany
Jakob Hoejmark	Intel, Germany

Local Organization Chairs

Kerstin Alexander	Intel, Germany
Martin Simon	Fraunhofer IKS, Germany
Miriam Friedmann	Fraunhofer IKS, Germany

Workshops Chair

Ilir Gashi	City University London, UK

Students Forum Chair

Marcello Cinque   Federico II University of Naples, Italy

Fast Abstracts Chair

Barbara Gallina   Mälardalen University, Sweden

Industry Track Chair

Wilfried Steiner   TTTech, Austria

Publication Chair

André Martin   Technische Universität Dresden, Germany

Publicity Chair

Paolo Lollini   University of Florence, Italy

Workshop on Dynamic Risk managEment for AutonoMousSystems (DREAMS)

Organizers

Rasmus Adler	Fraunhofer IESE, Germany
Daniel Schneider	Fraunhofer IESE, Germany
Philipp Schleiß	Fraunhofer IKS, Germany
Simon Burton	Fraunhofer IKS, Germany
Selma Saidi	TU Dortmund, Germany

Program Committee

Huascar Espinoza	CEA, France
Patrik Feth	Sick AG, Germany
Ibrahim Habli	Univeristy of York, UK
Richard Hawkins	Univeristy of York, UK
Ayhan Mehmed	TTTech Auto AG, Austria
Fabian Oboril	Intel, Germany
Yiannis Papadopoulos Koopmann	University of Hull, UK
Gordon Blair	Lancaster University, UK
Ganesh Pai	NASA, KBR, USA
Phil Kopmann	Carnegie Mellon University, USA
Eric Armengaud	Armengaud Innovate GmbH, Austria
Roman Gansch	Robert Bosch GmbH, Germany
Erwin Schoitsch	Austrian Institute of Technology, Austria

Workshop on Dependable SOlutions for Intelligent Electricity Distribution GRIds (DSOGRI)

Program Chairs

Nicola Nostro   Resiltech s.r.l., Italy
Rasmus Løvenstein Olsen   Aalborg University, Denmark
Hans-Peter Schwefel   GridData GmbH, Germany, and Aalborg
                                   University, Denmark

Program Committee

Cristina Alcaraz   University of Malaga, Spain
Magnus Almgren   Chalmers University, Sweden
Silvia Bonomi   University of Rome "La Sapienza", Italy
Filipe Caldeira   Polytechnic Institute of Viseu, Portugal
Geert Deconinck   KU Leuven, Belgium
Herman De Meer   University of Passau, Germany
Markus Duchon   Fortiss, Munich, Germany
Wilfried Elmenreich   University of Klagenfurt, Austria
Karsten Handrup   Kamstrup A/S, Denmark
Rune Hylsberg Jacobsen   Aarhus University, Denmark
Paolo Lollini   University of Florence, Italy
Henrique Madeira   Universidade de Coimbra, Portugal
Giulio Masetti   ISTI-CNR, Italy
Leonardo Montecchi   Universidade Estadual de Campinas, Brazil
Walter Schaffer   Salzburg Netz Gmbh, Austria
Kamal Shahid   Aalborg University, Denmark
Hamid Shaker   South Danish University, Denmark
Nuno Pedro Silva   Critical Software, Portugal
Dejan Vukobratovic   University of Novi Sad, Serbia
Christoph Winter   Salzburg AG, Austria

Workshop on Software Engineering for Resilient Systems (SERENE)

Program Chairs

Amel Bennaceur   The Open University, UK
Amleto Di Salle   University of L'Aquila, Italy

Steering Committee

Didier Buchs   University of Geneva, Switzerland
Henry Muccini   University of L'Aquila, Italy
Patrizio Pelliccione   Gran Sasso Science Institute, Italy, and Chalmers
                                   University of Technology|Gothenburg
                                   University, Sweden
Alexander Romanovsky   Newcastle University, UK
Elena Troubitsyna   KTH Royal Institute of Technology, Sweden

Program Committee

Marco Autili	University of L'Aquila, Italy
Georgios Bouloukakis	Télécom SudParis, France
Radu Calinescu	University of York, UK
Andrea Ceccarelli	University of Florence, Italy
Felicita Di Giandomenico	CNR-ISTI, Italy
Carlos Gavidia-Calderon	The Open University, UK
Nikolaos Georgantas	Inria, France
Simos Gerasimou	University of York, UK
Jeremie Guiochet	LAAS-CNRS, Université de Toulouse 3, France
Linas Laibinis	Vilnius University, Lithuania
Istvan Majzik	Budapest University of Technology and Economics, Hungary
Paolo Masci	National Institute of Aerospace, Langley Research Center, USA
Raffaela Mirandola	Politecnico di Milano, Italy
Henry Muccini	University of L'Aquila, Italy
Andras Pataricza	Budapest University of Technology and Economics (BME), Hungary
Patrizio Pelliccione	Gran Sasso Science Institute, Italy, and Chalmers University of Technology|Gothenburg University, Sweden
Cristina Seceleanu	Malardalen University, Sweden
Alin Stefanescu	University of Bucharest, Romania
Elena Troubitsyna	KTH Royal Institute of Technology, Sweden
Karthik Vaidhyanathan	University of L'Aquila, Italy
Marco Vieira	University of Coimbra, Portugal
Apostolos Zarras	University of Ioannina, Greece

Contents

Workshop on Software Engineering for Resilient Systems (SERENE)

Workshop on Dynamic Risk managEment for AutonoMous Systems (DREAMS)

Second Workshop on Dynamic Risk managEment for AutonoMous Systems (DREAMS)

Workshop Description

Autonomous systems (AS) have enormous potential and are bound to be a major driver in future economic and societal transformations. Their key trait is that they pursue and achieve their more or less explicitly defined goals independently and without human guidance or intervention. In contexts where safety or other critical properties need to be guaranteed, it is, however, hardly possible at present to exploit autonomous systems to their full potential. Unknowns and uncertainties are induced due to high complexity of autonomous behaviour, the utilised technology, and the volatile and highly complex system context in which AS operate. These characteristics render the base assumptions of established assurance methods (and standards) insufficient and make it necessary to investigate new approaches at runtime.

One promising approach for building dependable autonomous systems is to design such systems with the capability to identify, assess, and control risks. Implementing such a Dynamic Risk Management (DRM) technology entails many challenges concerning the necessary self-awareness and context awareness. On the one hand, powerful and thus complex self-awareness and context awareness are necessary to minimize risks, resolve conflicting objectives, and make acceptable trade-off decisions. On the other hand, the complexity of the models hinders the assurance of critical properties and prevents gaining sufficient confidence in DRM. DRM has the potential to not only enable certain types of systems or applications outright, but also to significantly increase the utility of already existing ones. This is due to the fact that by resolving unknowns and dealing with uncertainties at runtime, it will be possible to eliminate worst-case assumptions that are typically detrimental to a system's utility.

The DREAMS workshop intends to explore concepts and techniques for realising DRM. It invites experts, researchers, and practitioners to give presentations and take part in in-depth discussions about prediction models for risk identification, integration between strategic, tactical, and operational risk management, architectures for dynamic risk management, and validation & verification of dynamic risk management.

DREAMS aims at bringing together communities from diverse disciplines, such as safety engineering, runtime adaptation, system reconfiguration, predictive modelling, and control theory, and from different application domains such as automotive, healthcare, manufacturing, agriculture, and critical infrastructures.

Towards a Software Component to Perform Situation-Aware Dynamic Risk Assessment for Autonomous Vehicles

Jan Reich[1(✉)], Marc Wellstein[1], Ioannis Sorokos[1], Fabian Oboril[2], and Kay-Ulrich Scholl[2]

[1] Safety Engineering, Fraunhofer IESE, Kaiserslautern, Germany
{jan.reich,marc.wellstein,ioannis.sorokos}@iese.fraunhofer.de
[2] Intel Labs, Intel Corporation, Karlsruhe, Germany
{fabian.oboril,kay-ulrich.scholl}@intel.com

Abstract. Assuring an adequate level of safety is the key challenge for the approval of autonomous vehicles (AV). Dynamic Risk Assessment (DRA) enables AVs to assess the risk of the current situation instead of behaving according to worst-case expectations regarding all possible situations. While current DRA techniques typically predict the behavior of others based on observing kinematic states, Situation-Aware Dynamic Risk Assessment (SINADRA) uses probabilistic environmental knowledge about causal factors that indicate behavior changes *before* they occur. In this paper, we expand upon previous conceptual ideas and introduce an open-source Python software component that realizes the SINADRA pipeline including situation class detection, Bayesian network-based behavior intent prediction, trajectory distribution generation, and the final risk assessment. We exemplify the component's usage by estimating front vehicle braking risks in the CARLA AV simulator.

1 Introduction

Autonomous Vehicles (AVs) will transform our transportation business in many ways, and are seen as one of the major innovations for the next decade. However, there are still several challenges that need to be addressed before mass deployment is possible. One of these challenges is to solve the problem of Dynamic Risk Assessment (DRA). DRA enables AVs to analyze the (collision) risk of a traffic situation dynamically and plan its decisions accordingly, for example by selecting a risk-minimizing behavior to find the right balance between safety and availability. While humans perform such behavior implicitly, comprehensive algorithmic solutions for AVs are still missing. While a lot of simpler yet certifiable DRA solutions like Time-To-Collision (TTC) exist for predicting emergency braking maneuvers [2], they are not fit for operation in complex environmental situations, which AV need to face. The key reason for this is the situation-agnostic

The work presented in this paper was partially supported by the Intel Collaborative Research Institute ICRI SAVe (http://icri-save.de/).

approach aiming at using a few metrics covering all situations. However, the motion of traffic participants is heavily influenced by the driving environment in reality and therefore the assumptions of these models often do not hold. In order to predict human traffic behavior more accurate, environmental influencing factors other than the kinematic state need to be taken into account, favorably in a probabilistic way to explicitly incorporate uncertainty related to the factors. If behavior intents and respective future trajectories are predicted more accurately, trajectory-based risk metric accuracy is improved, too.

For this purpose, in this work, we present both the conceptual concretization and the software realization of *Situation-Aware* Dynamic Risk Assessment (SINADRA) introduced in [5], an approach that aims at improving risk assessment accuracy by employing situational awareness for behavior prediction. SINADRA uses probabilistic Bayesian network (BN) models to infer behavior intents of other traffic participants based on dynamically measured environmental cues. These behavior intents are transformed into trajectory distributions by using behavior-specific motion models. Given the predicted future positions of traffic participants and a planned ego trajectory, probabilistic risk metrics such as [1] can determine the risk of executing the planned ego trajectory in the current situation. In contrast to [5], where BNs were envisioned to be used to predict the collision risk, the SINADRA concept has been refined in that BNs are now used to predict behavior intents only, followed by the trajectory generation and risk assessment steps. We realized the SINADRA computation pipeline as a Python software component and coupled it with the CARLA simulator[1].

This paper describes the functionality, structure, and usage of this software component and contributes by facilitating further research in the area of situation-aware dynamic risk assessment. Apart from presenting the internals of SINADRA, we show in principle how SINADRA can also be integrated into typical AV systems. The software component's source code is available as open source at GitHub[2]. In the long term, SINADRA shall become an utility measure that proactively avoids interventions of certified safety checkers through intelligent behavior prediction inspired by human cognition processes.

In Sect. 2, the conceptual ideas behind SINADRA are explained as the basis for understanding the architectural structure and sub-components of the software component. Afterwards, we elaborate on the technical details of the implementation in Sect. 3 before demonstrating the usage and output of the SINADRA component in a front vehicle braking scenario in Sect. 4. Section 5 concludes the work and outlines future research directions.

2 Situation-Aware Dynamic Risk Assessment (SINADRA)

Situational awareness is a key ingredient for balancing AV safety and availability because risk assessment accuracy depends on correct (critical) behavior predic-

---

[1] CARLA AV Simulator: https://carla.org/.
[2] SINADRA GitHub Repository: https://github.com/JaRei/sinadra.

tion, which is highly specific to the current environmental situation in a versatile traffic environment. The aim of SINADRA is to improve risk assessment accuracy by providing probabilistic behavior intent prediction models that imitate how humans infer behavior intents based on environmental cues. More specifically, SINADRA predicts probabilities of unwanted events and thereby contributes to risk assessment, while it does not predict consequences of such events.

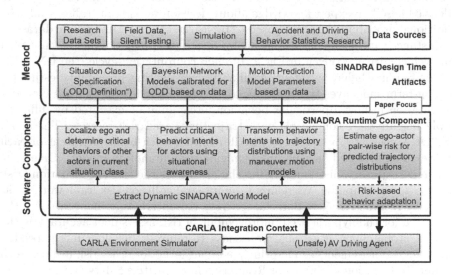

Fig. 1. Overview of the SINADRA architecture.

The SINADRA pipeline contains four components (orange in Fig. 1) that return a risk estimate per ego-actor pair based on the *Dynamic SINADRA World Model*, which represents relevant information from the ego environment and the *AV Driving Agent*. It provides information from the environment (a) for ego localization and traffic actor role classification in the context of situation classes (e.g. actor position, movement direction, actor type), (b) about situation-influencing factors being relevant for predicting (critical) behavior intents (e.g. weather conditions, road topology, past behavior) and (c) to transform behavior intents into trajectories by considering the kinematic state. In addition, the ego *AV Driving Agent* provides information about its currently planned trajectory to support pair-wise risk assessment with the planned ego trajectory and predicted actor trajectories.

The first step is the localization of the ego in a situation class in an operational design domain (ODD). The SINADRA-specific ODD definition can be understood as a graph of situation classes that the ego traverses during driving. Each situation class defines a set of ego behaviors, a set of actor roles relative to the ego, and a set of environmental conditions influencing the likelihood of behavior intents for the other actors. A situation class captures modular properties of the environmental situation required for determining the relevance of other actors in terms of behaviors being critical for the ego vehicle. For instance, the situation class single lane following models actor roles and associated behavior possibilities for a front vehicle, a back vehicle and vehicles on the other road direction.

Behavior intents can be modeled as joint probability distributions of causal behavior influence factors being assumed to be distributed probabilistic, too. For each behavior intent associated with a classified actor role, SINADRA uses Bayesian networks (BN) to capture the relationships. The BN structure is derived based on expert knowledge about decision-making in traffic, while the conditional probabilities are supposed to be learned from ODD-specific datasets. For instance, an exemplary structure for a BN to predict brake intents of a front vehicle driver is given in Fig. 2. In each computation cycle, the BN inference determines behavior *intent* likelihoods representing probability estimates for long-term maneuver types. However, the behavior intents neither consider the variation in how a particular behavior intent may be executed by different people nor are they compatible with trajectory-based risk metrics. Therefore, SINADRA generates a trajectory distribution for each behavior intent of each considered actor based on sampling behavior-specific motion models. Given the predicted trajectory distributions for the actors in the current situation, risk metrics can be computed. We realized the integral collision risk framework [1] as a concrete risk metric. Note that the concrete risk metric is exchangeable, as the key reason for the hypothesized improvement in risk assessment accuracy is the usage of probabilistic situational awareness to improve behavior intent prediction. Thus, improvements can in principle be achieved for other risk metrics such as Time-To-Collision (TTC) [3] or Responsibility Sensitive Safety (RSS) [7], too.

The SINADRA output shall be used within the *AV Driving Agent* to enable the nominal driving policy to avoid critical situations proactively, i.e. to make decision. There are two ways to achieve that: Either the policy's planning space is constrained by SINADRA (e.g. with *risk maps* [1]) or the planned trajectory is verified segment-wise requiring knowledge about reactive capabilities and criteria for risk acceptance (e.g. [4]). Since the primary purpose of SINADRA is to avoid safety checker interventions (e.g. minimum risk maneuvers) and thereby improve utility, we currently work towards providing constraints to trajectory planners. Thus, a simpler and certifiable yet less foresighted safety checker is assumed to be operating in parallel.

3   SINADRA Python Implementation in CARLA

The SINADRA library provides an open-source Python 3 implementation of functionality required to perform probabilistic and situation-aware dynamic risk assessment according to Fig. 1. The library has been integrated with the open-source CARLA simulator to enable SINADRA research experiments in a simulation environment. SINADRA integrates with CARLA by providing a CARLA Python client script containing the main loop that dynamically populates the *SINADRA World Model* and orchestrates the SINADRA computation work. The SINADRA operation in CARLA is currently built on the assumption that environmental scenarios are specified (currently two-lane following scenarios) and started with the CARLA *Scenario Runner* plug-in and the ego vehicle is driven via an automated driving policy. The component comes with a set of configuration parameters for varying situation class detection conditions, trajectory generators, risk model, prediction horizon, and time step.

ODD Specification and Situation Class Detection. The actor situation class detection package classifies both ego and ego-near actors into roles within the current situation. Each situation class specifies a set of conditions that must hold for an actor to assume a particular role in that class (e.g., the role *side vehicle* must be in a lane adjacent to the ego vehicle and drive in the same direction relative to the ego). Technically, the actor situation class detection contains a situation class state machine that specifies the operational domain in terms of an abstract graph relating situation classes in a map (e.g., Town03) and their topological relationship.

Behavior Intent Prediction with Bayesian Networks. The Bayesian network (BN) Python module for predicting situation-specific behavior likelihoods contains both design time and runtime aspects. The open-source Python library pgmpy[3] is used as a runtime inference library. At design time, the component supports the generation of pgmpy-conformant BN runtime representations and evidence data connector classes suitable for runtime inference. At runtime, the component allows BN-based behavior intent prediction for the scene actors in each simulation step. Multiple BNs for the behaviors of multiple actors are computed simultaneously in each time step. SINADRA supports the automated transformation from BNs modeled graphically in the widely used GeNIe[4] tool (.xdsl) into pgmpy BNs (.xmlbif). Furthermore, for each BN a specific configuration Python class is generated that decouples the BN specification from the BN data provision. This class enables specifying which dynamic evidence from the simulator is mapped to which BN node and which value ranges are mapped to which discrete node state. Finally, the BN model is mapped to a particular actor role in a particular situation class, e.g., a BN for cut-in prediction for a vehicle actor driving on the left adjacent lane relative to the ego in a lane-following situation class. Note that using a graphical modeling tool such as GeNIe is helpful for BN verification and validation being especially important, when explainability is required as in the safety or utility context.

Trajectory Distribution Generation. To transform behavior intents to trajectory distributions, SINADRA supports respective generators for three longitudinal behaviors and one lateral one:

1. Constant acceleration, adapted from the 'Follow Road' model in [6] (p. 5). A special case is emergency braking considering a constant maximum deceleration.
2. Brake for a known static target such as a red traffic light or a stop line, adapted from the 'Target Brake' model in [6] (p. 6).

---

[3] https://github.com/pgmpy/pgmpy.
[4] https://www.bayesfusion.com/genie/.

3. Intelligent Driver Model (IDM) [8], which combines free cruising without a front vehicle and maintaining a target time gap to a front vehicle.
4. Lane Change with a constant average velocity. Generated trajectories follow a cubic Bézier spline generated between the initial vehicle position and the desired endpoint, with automatically generated intermediate control points.

Risk Metric Computation. For the last step in the SINADRA pipeline, risk must be assessed for the predicted future situation represented by the generated trajectory distributions of other vehicles. For this purpose, we adapted the integral collision probability framework proposed in [1]. The employed probabilistic risk metric is situation-agnostic, i.e., it operates on arbitrary trajectory distributions. The integral collision risk is defined as the cumulative probability of having a lateral or longitudinal distance between the ego and another actor smaller than zero at a particular time instant. In SINADRA, the integral collision risk of each ego-actor trajectory distribution pair is computed. If an actor has different possible behavior intents in the current situation, a risk score is computed for the trajectory distribution of *each* behavior intent. The risk accuracy improvement achieved by SINADRA comes in only at this last stage, where the total integral collision risk is computed by *weighting the individual risk scores* based on the behavior intent likelihoods inferred from the BNs.

4   Usage Example: Front Vehicle Braking Risk

This section explains with an example the usage of the SINADRA component in two variations of a vehicle following scenario (see Fig. 3). The blue ego vehicle is following the red front vehicle (FV), which approaches another green front vehicle that has a lower traveling speed than ego and FV. The goal is to assess the integral collision risk between the ego and the red front vehicle in both scenarios. Figure 2 shows an excerpt of the BN used to predict the braking behavior intents of the front vehicle.

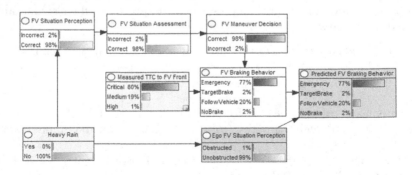

Fig. 2. Example Bayesian network for braking behavior prediction.

The nodes can be classified as a) the causal chain of the actor's decision-making process (white), b) the dynamic evidences being retrieved from sensor readings/perception stack (green), and c) influences limiting the ego's capability to observe the influences on the actor's decision-making process (orange). The green evidence nodes are chosen for illustration purposes only, i.e. in reality there are more environmental influence features taken into account for each white node. In addition, uncertainties regarding perceived features can be directly incorporated into the BN model out-of-the-box (e.g., Measured TTC node). Note that Time-To-Collision (TTC) is not used here as a risk metric to capture ego behavior risk, but to model the red front vehicle driver's risk-aware decision-making regarding braking.

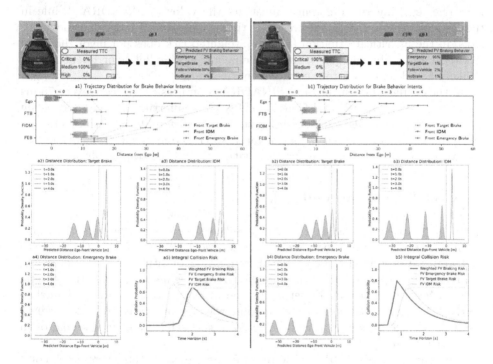

Fig. 3. Situation-aware front vehicle braking risk assessment with SINADRA in uncritical (left) and critical scenario (right).

Figure 3 shows the intermediate outcomes of the SINADRA pipeline in the example. The variation between both scenarios is induced by having medium (left) and critical (right) TTC values between the red and green vehicles. The BN inference results in different relative braking behavior intent likelihoods for emergency braking and following the green vehicle with moderate braking expectations. Subplots a1 and b1 show the predicted trajectory distributions for the possible behavior intents over time. Note that the Intelligent Driver Model (IDM) combines the *Follow vehicle* and *No brake* (i.e., road cruise) behavior intents.

The ego trajectory is constructed by assuming a constant speed in this example, while in reality the trajectory would be provided by the ego trajectory planner. Subplots a2–a4) and b2–b4) show the distance distribution after combining the ego trajectory distribution with each actor's trajectory distribution. The red area below the probability density functions at different times indicates the cumulative probability of both vehicles being at the same position at the same time (i.e., crashed), which is the distance-based risk criterion used in [1]. Interesting to note is that in a4), a critical situation is predicted to happen at around 1.0 s due to assumed emergency braking, while in a2), the critical situation happens only at around 2.0 s. The final integral collision risk assessment is shown in plots a5) and b5), where the separate integral collision risks of front vehicle behavior intents (dashed) are weighted with the behavior likelihoods inferred from the BN. The resulting risk differences illustrate the value of SINADRA: While in the critical situation (b5), the weighted risk is close to all individual behavior risks, in the uncritical situation (a5), the weighted risk does not favor the high-risk score from the emergency braking behavior, as this behavior intent is very unlikely based on the current environmental situation.

In the current implementation, SINADRA computes a risk score every 75 ms on average, on a typical Intel Core i5 7600K CPU inferring braking and cut-in behavior BNs in parallel and generating trajectory distributions with 20 samples for each of the four different behavior intents. The component predicts the risk for two actors over a 4.0 s time horizon with a 0.2 s time step resolution.

5   Conclusion and Outlook

In this paper, we introduced an open-source Python software component for performing Situation-Aware Dynamic Risk Assessment (SINADRA) in CARLA. To that end, we described the conceptual foundation of situation class detection, behavior intent prediction, trajectory distribution generation, and risk assessment in Sect. 2. Important decisions for the implementation were explained in Sect. 3. The SINADRA component outcome was demonstrated in Sect. 4, where the front vehicle braking risk was predicted in two vehicle following scenarios in the CARLA simulator.

We believe the SINADRA software component enables the AV research community to experiment with advanced situational awareness for behavior prediction and risk assessment. Concretely, future work will use the software component as a basis to perform sensitivity analyses to evaluate, which environmental factors have high impact on collision risk and to automatically search for situations, where learned BN model intent predictions deviate from expert expectations. Technically, we plan to extend the component to be applicable in a wider range of scenarios, such as intersections, and include pedestrians as actors considered for intent prediction.

References

1. Eggert, J.: Risk estimation for driving support and behavior planning in intelligent vehicles. at-Automatisierungstechnik **66**(2), 119–131 (2018)
2. Feth, P.: Dynamic behavior risk assessment for autonomous systems. Dissertation, Technical University Kaiserslautern, Germany (2020)
3. Horst, R.: Time-to-collision as a cue for decision-making in braking. Vision in Vehicles-III (1991)
4. Pek, C., Manzinger, S., Koschi, M., Althoff, M.: Using online verification to prevent autonomous vehicles from causing accidents. Nat. Mach. Intell. **2**(9), 518–528 (2020). https://doi.org/10.1038/s42256-020-0225-y
5. Reich, J., Trapp, M.: SINADRA: towards a framework for assurable situation-aware dynamic risk assessment of autonomous vehicles. In: 16th European Dependable Computing Conference (EDCC) (2020). https://doi.org/10.1109/EDCC51268.2020.00017
6. Schreier, M., Willert, V., Adamy, J.: An integrated approach to maneuver-based trajectory prediction and criticality assessment in arbitrary road environments. IEEE Trans. Intell. Transp. Syst. **17**(10), 2751–2766 (2016)
7. Shalev-Shwartz, S., Shammah, S., Shashua, A.: On a formal model of safe and scalable self-driving cars. arXiv:1708.06374 (2017)
8. Treiber, M., Hennecke, A., Helbing, D.: Congested traffic states in empirical observations and microscopic simulations. Phys. Rev. E **62**(2), 1805 (2000)

Service-Oriented Reconfiguration in Systems of Systems Assured by Dynamic Modular Safety Cases

Carsten Thomas[1]([⊠]) [iD], Elham Mirzaei[1] [iD], Björn Wudka[1] [iD], Lennart Siefke[2] [iD],
and Volker Sommer[2] [iD]

[1] HTW Berlin, University of Applied Sciences, Computer Engineering, Berlin,
Germany
{carsten.thomas,elham.mirzaei,bjoern.wudka}@htw-berlin.de
[2] Beuth University of Applied Sciences Berlin, Computer Engineering, Berlin,
Germany
{lennart.siefke,sommer}@beuth-hochschule.de

Abstract. The drive for automation in industry and transport results in an increasing demand for cooperative systems that form cyber-physical systems of systems. One of the characteristic features of such systems is dynamic reconfiguration, which facilitates emergent behavior to respond to internal variations as well as to environmental changes. By means of cooperation, systems of systems can achieve greater efficiency regarding fulfillment of their goals. These goals are not limited to performance, but must also include safety aspects to assure a system of systems to operate safely in various configurations. In this paper, we present a reconfiguration approach which includes consideration of dynamic modular safety cases. During operation, configuration of system of systems will adapt to changes, selecting the most appropriate service composition from the set of possible compositions derived from blueprints. Variations of service compositions lead to changes in the associated safety cases, which are evaluated at run-time and taken into account during configuration selection. With this approach, safe operation of cyber-physical systems of systems with run-time reconfiguration can be guaranteed.

Keywords: Systems of systems · Dynamic modular safety cases · Service-oriented reconfiguration · Blueprints · Service-oriented architecture

1 Introduction

In this paper, we consider systems of systems (SoS) as defined in [1], that consist of a large number of systems or agents, that are contextualized in an interactive

This research was funded by the Berlin Institute for Applied Research (IFAF) within the SiReSS-project, and by the German Ministry for Education and Research in frame of the ITEA3 research project CyberFactory#1 under funding ID 01IS18061D.

R. Adler et al. (Eds.): EDCC 2021 Workshops, CCIS 1462, pp. 12–29, 2021.
https://doi.org/10.1007/978-3-030-86507-8_2

environment, and that manifest emergent behavior. The constituting systems are goal-oriented with incomplete information at any given moment and interact among themselves and with the environment. Specifically, we focus on cyber-physical systems (CPS) [2] and open SoS [3], i.e. SoS with joining and leaving constituting systems. Examples of such SoS are road vehicle platoons, virtually coupled trains in transportation, or fleets of autonomous transport vehicles in a factory. To be able to adapt to changes in their environment or changes in constituting systems (such as system failures) as well as adapting and optimizing SoS performance during operation, SoS should have the ability to reconfigure themselves dynamically at run-time. Dynamic reconfiguration is the capability of SoS to change their composition and structure, typically without planned intervention [4]. Reconfiguration approaches can be divided into *Predefined*, *Constrained* and *Unconstrained Selection* [5]. Whilst being the most complex approach, *Unconstrained Selection* provides the highest level of flexibility and optimally supports open SoS.

Increasingly, open SoS are applied in safety critical environments. Assuring their safety is essential, also in context of reconfiguration at run-time. This is challenging due to the potentially huge number of configurations that result from SoS complexity and openness, and the impossibility to establish complete safety analysis evidence for all configurations during design-time. Traditional approaches such as a design-time-created safety case (SC) are not sufficient in this context. In the coming chapters we will present the approach of Service-oriented Reconfiguration with the integration of Dynamic Modular Safety Cases (DMSC) to be able to reconstruct safe configurations at run-time. Therefore, we will first take a look at related work (Sect. 2) on dynamic reconfiguration and safety. In Sect. 3, we describe the principles of dynamic reconfiguration based on a service-oriented architecture, and introduce the blueprint concept as a step towards *Unconstrained Selection*. Further, in Sect. 4, we explain the use of DMSC for the assurance of potential new SoS configurations at run-time. In Sect. 5, we apply these concepts on an automated factory scenario to illustrate the process of reconfiguration and safety case evaluation using an example. Finally, in Sect. 6, we summarize our approaches and outline further steps.

2 Related Work

2.1 Dynamic Reconfiguration

Reconfiguration is the possibility to change a system of interest (e.g., an SoS) regarding its internal structure, functionality, and properties. Through reconfiguration, systems are able to adapt to changing environment and system-internal variations such as malfunctions, ideally preserving or even improving key properties such as safety and performance. One of the process schemes applied reconfiguration is the one described by Bradbury et al. [5]. This scheme consists of four steps: initiation, selection, implementation and assessment. By initiation, systems monitor themselves and their environment. In MAPE-K (Monitor-Analyze-Plan-Execution Knowledge) loop [6] the initiation is described with more detail by monitoring and analyze. In this context, Monitoring is used to detect changes and Analyzing is used to identify the impact of change. Therefore Analyzing is in use of a database which provides system related data. After successful initiation, a description of the initiation event is passed to the next step to provide the informational basis for configuration selection. For this step, the scheme distinguishes between (1) *Predefined Selection*, (2) *Constrained Selection*, and (3) *Unconstrained Selection*. The approaches presented in most papers are restricted to *Constrained Selection* using predefined sets of configurations [7–10]. Other approaches concentrating in cyber-physical systems reconfiguration [11,12]. In the paper of Zeadally et al. [13] cyber-physical system adaptation approaches of the past years are discussed. A general solution for *Unconstrained selection* is currently not available. To select configurations, Kosmalska [14] describes flexible reconfiguration based on situation. There, reconfiguration is operating in constraints of safety, reliability and performance goals. These evaluation is necessary to calculate effectiveness in context of situation for a variety of configurations. Sillmann et al. [15] presents a method for SoS to evaluate configurations of applications in a smart house. Other papers evaluate and optimize single operating systems by pre-defined configurations [16–18]. For safety-critical applications, also the safety properties of potential new configurations must be evaluated as part of the selection process. In Sect. 2.2, we present current approaches for this evaluation. When selection is completed, the changes will be implemented into the system. By the step of integration, system have to handle blackout time while systems change configurations. The approach of Schneider [19] is aiming to minimize these time by using a short handshake between services that have to be started and stopped. Finally, if the implementation is done, the assessment will be performed. In the model described above, the system checks in the assessment step solely the successful implementation of the configuration change. But it is also possible to change the steps in their order to directly determined whether an intended target configuration fulfills the given goals of the system. In summary, related research indicates that reconfiguration approaches employing *Constrained Selection* are well developed, but these approaches do not yet offer the flexible and safe reconfiguration scheme which is required for the dynamic reconfiguration of open SoS at run-time.

2.2 Safety Assurance

Safety cases (SC) are used in several industries to document safety evidence "in form of an explained and well-founded structured argument to clearly communicate that the system is acceptably safe to operate in a given context" [20]. Modular safety cases (MSC), in particular were introduced to cope with system complexity by breaking down safety arguments into modules, in order to reduce cost and impact of changes during the system life-cycle [21], whilst dynamic safety cases (DSC) were developed to bridge the gap between assumptions taken at design-time and properties of the realized system becoming apparent at run-time [22]. In order to benefit from both approaches, dynamic modular safety cases (DMSC) have been proposed as a means to master challenges such as complexity and dynamic nature of SoS [23], a concept that we will further elaborate in this paper. Within this paper we use the Goal Structuring Notation (GSN) [24] to construct SC arguments during design-time. According to the GSN standard, Goal(G) is indicated by rectangle, presenting safety goal; Strategy(S) is indicated by a parallelogram, describing the inference that exists between a goal and its supporting goal(s); Solution(Sl) is indicated by circle, presenting a reference to an evidence item presented as Sl. Many approaches can be found in literature that address open challenges such as automation, re-evaluation after change and run-time assessments, change impact propagation and dynamic construction of SC for SoS. In the context of MSC approaches, one key aspect is the definition and handling of borders and relations between modules. Contracts were introduced as a means to capture such dependencies between SC modules [25–29]. A description of systematic approaches how to apply contracts is proposed in [30, 31] which, was further developed in [32] proposing a maintenance framework to facilitate the change management for SC at design-time. This work is followed by [33] using safety contracts to verify design assumptions at run-time, observing failure rates in the operational life. This approach is not yet fully automated and does not cover structural changes in in SoS. However, in [34] the application of MSC in Industry 4.0 is proposed, highlighting the open challenges within such SoS. Correspondingly, there is ongoing research focusing on the evolution of the DSC approach. ENTRUST (ENgineering of TRUstworthy Self-adaptive sofTware) proposes assurance processes to develop trustworthy self-adaptive software, while combining design-time and run-time modeling and verification activities [35]. Many DSC-related research proposes initial steps toward automated construction and assessments of SC [36–40].

Whist some of these approaches consider DSC and some focus on MSC, there is less work trying to combine the two concepts to overcome the challenges for reconfiguration of SoS during run-time. One of the combined approaches proposes modular conditional safety certificates (ConSerts), and is built on a series of formalized guarantee-demand relationships that can be composed and evaluated during run-time [41]. However, there are some limitation associated to this approach regarding dynamic variability in particular in supporting dynamic reconfiguration in the SoS structure. In this approach the adaptive behavior of systems has been constrained to pre-engineered adaptation. Nevertheless, many work has been published afterwards towards coping with this open captured limitation [42–44]. More developments towards formalising the SC and monitoring safety elements were described in these works. Furthermore, the application of MSC within SoS [45] is described supporting semi-automated and fully automated approaches. Within this method, SoS will either transit into a degraded mode for a certain time and notify the system causing the problem, or the cooperation with the other system is terminated in case they can not fulfill the safety requirements during the failure mode. However, the abstract interaction between safety and performance goals is not described in this approach.

Despite all significant progress regarding SC construction, maintenance and assessment, SC are not yet sufficiently formalized to support full automation of these tasks, and application of the techniques at run-time within SoS. In the context of reconfiguration and system change, the semi-automated approaches proposed so far provide insight on expected change impact regarding safety. However, in most of these approaches the final decision mainly must be reviewed or verified by an engineer. For assuring safety within reconfiguration of SoS at run-time, a fully automated approach is required which can support the adaptive interaction between safety and performance goals at run-time. In our work, we build on the available MSC and DSC techniques and extend them towards an approach that lends itself to support automated safety assessment throughout SoS reconfiguration at run-time.

3 Service-Oriented Reconfiguration

3.1 Service-Oriented Architecture

Our work focuses on spontaneously connecting systems, interacting with each other and with their environment, which reveals emergent behavior as an SoS. Service-oriented architectures (SoA) are a suitable means to design and develop software for such SoS [46], supporting software modularization and interoperability between systems [47]. Services are functional software modules which are loosely coupled with clearly defined interfaces. Furthermore, they do not need to know each other but only their interfaces, which they consume or provide. A service can consume and provide multiple interfaces. Using the discovery pattern, available services of constituting systems and their states can be discovered and observed at run-time. Services publish their state and health data to the discovery component. We adapt the discovery pattern to be suitable for decentralized and spontaneously connecting systems. There is one component in each system performing discovery pattern called SystemDiscovery. Each service belongs to one system and registers itself to the local SystemDiscovery. The SystemDiscovery components of the different systems exchange their lists of local service descriptions and build up catalogs of available services. Using this pattern, available systems and their abilities can be detected and observed at run-time.

Cooperative functionality (resulting in emerging behavior of the SoS) is designed and implemented with multiple services. As each service implements a defined limited functionality, services are composed to provide more complex functionality. A composition of services is a set of services which are connected with their interfaces. In addition, our concept implements an orchestration pattern: The services do not become active by themselves but are activated and deactivated by the Reconfiguration component. First, the Reconfiguration component of an individual system establishes a configuration of basic services and service compositions based on the available services in the own system and other systems of the SoS. Afterwards, each Reconfiguration component orchestrates the services of the own system according to the plan and services get connected across the boundaries of the individual systems.

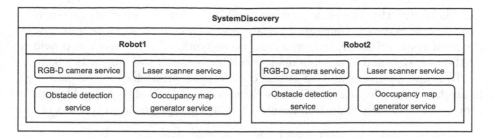

Fig. 1. An example SystemDiscovery component with a catalog of services from two different systems.

3.2   Blueprints and Configurations

Most approaches for reconfiguration are using configuration trees that represent all possible configurations. Configuration trees are a concept in line with the *Constrained Selection* approach that is well suited for systems and SoS with restricted variability. Open SoS require more flexibility for reconfiguration, as their constituting systems are not known at design-time (neither concerning their number, nor necessarily regarding their type and capabilities). To enable initial steps towards supporting *Unconstrained Selection*, we proposed *Blueprints* as a new concept to describe the variability of open SoS and to implicitly define all possible configurations of the SoS [48].

Blueprints define needed features of services, such as purpose, interfaces (input and outputs), and structural composition. The blueprint concept is similar to a class concept in object-oriented programming languages, as it implements the following concepts:

- **Inheritance:** A specific blueprint can be a specialization of a more generic blueprint (e.g., ultrasonic distance sensor blueprint and infrared distance sensor blueprint are both derived from the distance sensor blueprint).
- **Composition:** Blueprints may represent basic services, or service compositions. In the latter case, the blueprint specification contains information on the required blueprint components and the internal interconnections.
- **Instantiation:** Configuration of services are built by creating instances of services at run-time (e.g., two laser distance sensors of the same type built into a specific test robot together with the software service that reads the values from these sensors are two instances of the infrared distance sensor blueprint).

In order to build-up a new service configuration, a blueprint must be instantiated. This can be done by creating an instance of a basic service that matches the blueprint (like the laser distance sensor service instances mentioned above), or by selecting a service composition blueprint as a specialization of the required blueprint, and iteratively instantiating and connecting the components of this service composition blueprint.

Combining the blueprint concept and the concept of SystemDiscovery explained in Sect. 3.1, configurations are not restricted to services available in the local system. Rather, blueprints can be instantiated using services provided by the own system and services made available by other systems in the SoS.

To support implementation of this concept, blueprints have to be described in machine readable language. To ease definition, we decided to define blueprints using a text based specification format. A blueprint specification consists of

- blueprint name and (optionally) inheritance information
- (optionally, if not inherited from a more general blueprint) interface definition (inputs and outputs)
- (optionally, if it describes a service composition blueprint) composition information, listing the constituting components and their interconnections.

In addition, blueprint specifications may contain information related to the safety assurance concept which are introduced and described in more detail in Sect. 4. In Fig. 2 an example of blueprint is presented.

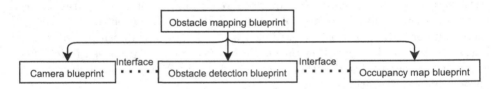

Fig. 2. Obstacle mapping service composition blueprint composed of camera service blueprint, obstacle detection blueprint and occupancy map blueprint

3.3 Reconfiguration Sequence

The reconfiguration sequence is used to create possible new configurations and to select and implement the most suitable of these configurations. It is based on the concepts of SoA and blueprints introduced in Sects. 3.1 and 3.2. This combination forms the concept of Service-oriented Reconfiguration (SoR).

Following the reconfiguration process scheme introduced in Sect. 2.1, the SoR sequence starts with the *Initiation* step. In our case, a change in the availability of services, observed by the SystemDiscovery component, will be a trigger event for reconfiguration. Such change may result from a previously available service becoming unavailable due to failure, or from systems entering or leaving the SoS. Nevertheless, reconfiguration could also be triggered by monitoring components which detect deviations of systems behavior or changes in the environment of the SoS.

The next step, *Selection*, is the key step in our process scheme. Within this step, there are several sub-steps:

- **Creation of all possible configurations:** The top-most blueprint is selected, and the set of all possible configurations is created by instantiating the variability embedded in the hierarchy of service composition blueprints. This process uses the information on the services actually available in the SoS, an information that is provided by the SystemDiscovery component. The hierarchical structures of service composition blueprints are described by linking basic and/or composition blueprints, and applying the inheritance concept to allow using specializations of more general blueprints as valid components in service compositions.
- **Configuration validation:** The set of all valid configurations are selected from the set of possible configurations. In our case, this validation is done by re-evaluating the SC of the possible configurations at run-time, and deselecting those configurations that do not meet the safety goals defined for the top-most blueprint (see Sect. 4 for details).
- **Configuration evaluation:** All configurations in the set of valid configurations are evaluated regarding their performance merits, and the most suitable configuration is selected. Performance evaluation is using predefined goals and evaluation functions to evaluate the configurations. For each configuration, the Reconfiguration component recursively collects the information required to compute the performance values, traversing the hierarchy and receiving - with support of the SystemDiscovery component - information related to performance properties for each individual service instance that is part of the configuration. Based on the received information, the Reconfiguration component compares the goal satisfaction. Finally, the best performing valid configuration is chosen. This sub-step implicitly implements the *Assessment* step mentioned in Sect. 2.1.

By means of the *Implementation* step, the selected configuration is integrated into the system. First, to avoid duplicating service processes, the Reconfiguration component stops all services which are part of the previously active configuration and are not former needed for the new configuration. Subsequently, the services associated to the selected configuration will be activated by the Reconfiguration component. Activating a service is performed by starting the processes of a service and afterwards connecting the service interfaces according to the blueprint specification. In case the selected configuration involves also services from another system within the SoS, the Reconfiguration component of that other system must support the configuration implementation by starting the relevant services and assisting in connecting the interfaces.

4 Safe Reconfiguration Using Dynamic Modular Safety Cases

In the DMSC approach, we strictly distinguish the handling of SC at design-time and run-time. In general, the SC are constructed at design-time, based on the hazard analysis, safety requirements and evidence supporting the safety arguments, by defining top safety goals and decomposing them into sub-goals that are supported by evidences. As this work involves steps which today cannot be automated, it is performed by experts with support of engineering specialists from various fields.

As discussed earlier, SC may be modularized to ease their re-construction once a component of a system changes. This concept is essential for the application of SC in context of SoS and SoR at run-time. In the context of SoR, we decompose system SC arguments into connected SC sub-modules based on the SoA. For each blueprint, there might be one or more SC modules documenting the structured safety arguments related to specific safety goals. Thus, we decompose the SC into modules based on blueprint services. The resulting service-oriented SC modules can now be used to compose system-level safety arguments for a given configuration of services, even if this configuration involves services of another system. Similarly, SoS-level safety arguments can be constructed utilizing these SC modules.

Decomposing SC arguments into modules substantially eases the construction of safety arguments in SoS. Still the step of re-constructing and integrating the related arguments is necessary to assess the safety of the entire system or SoS. In our approach, we clarify boundaries and dependencies between the SC modules using the concept of contracts. In traditional MSC approaches, contracts are the main means to specify interfaces between SC modules facilitating impact analysis upon any changes. For our purpose - assuring safety during reconfiguration at run-time - contracts must be formalized in a machine-comprehensible manner to facilitate integration of different modules at run-time. To formalize the contracts as the element that will be checked at run-time, the safety engineer verifies all the goals as well as their required solutions at design-time. In this process, the properties connected to these safety elements are formalized and associated with the respective blueprint (see Sect. 3.2):

- For blueprints describing basic services, the associated SC modules guarantee certain safety-related properties (e.g., the safety integrity level of a component defined as qualitative property, or a sensor as instance of the distance measurement service blueprint having a certain maximum failure rate defined as quantitative property). In SC terms, these modules are terminal nodes in the SC module hierarchy (i.e., solutions) and contain evidence for the structured SC argument.
- For blueprints describing service compositions, the associated SC module provide guarantees regarding a specific safety goal, if the constituting services of the service composition blueprint provide certain assumed guarantees. The link between the guarantees expected from the constituting services and the guarantee provided by the service composition is made through the SC strategy associated to the module.

In order to define the interfaces amongst dependent SC modules within contracts, we define these relations as: (1) *Assume*: Specific safety-related properties that are assumed to be provided by the referenced modules lower in the SC hierarchy. (2) *Guarantee*: Specific safety-related properties that are guaranteed to other modules higher in the SC hierarchy. With such a definitions, we can establish the connections between the higher level modules and the lower level modules by capturing the SC argument dependencies within single systems and across systems within SoS. The contracts concept allows to construct the complete SC of a system or SoS from the SC modules associated to its constituting systems and services, and to assess the top-level safety goals in an automated way. The latter task is done by traversing top-down and bottom-up through the constructed complete SC, and by combining the SC guarantees provided by the services involved in service compositions in the manner defined by the SC strategies associated to these service compositions.

This method of constructing or re-constructing SC from SC modules and automatically assessing the compliance with top-level safety goals is restricted to SC aspects that can be formalized in a machine-comprehensible manner. Whilst this may be perceived as a limitation, many cases can be covered by the following method: An evidence for a safety-related property is assessed by an engineer at design-time, and the result of this check is documented as machine-comprehensible information associated to a basic service as a SC solution (e.g., the above-mentioned examples of compliance to a certain development safety standard would be coded as a Boolean value, and the sensor failure rate as a numerical probability value). The service composition blueprint, in turn, is associated to a SC strategy expressed as a function that takes the qualitative and/or quantitative guarantees of the constituting services as inputs and combines them to compute the result valid for the service composition. During SC assessment, this result is then compared with the assumption that the service composition has regarding the guarantees of the constituting services.

To ease the assessment process, we distinguish two values for each of the SC-related properties: (1) *Guaranteed value*: The maximum tolerated value for that property defined at design-time that must not be violated at run-time. (2) *Actual value*: The recomputed value that may vary at run-time as a result of changes in the system or SoS. This distinction allows us to stop early on the reassessment of a SC if we are only interested in the fact if the safety goal is met, and not in the actual value computed for the safety goal. For selecting the subset of valid configurations from the set of possible configurations, this is exactly the case. Therefore, bottom-up re-assessment of a SC can be halted as soon as an assumption associated to a service composition is confirmed as valid. Since in this case the service composition can keep its guarantee to the services higher in the composition hierarchy, all higher assumptions defined at design-time are implicitly confirmed as valid, and the top-level safety goal can be confirmed as being met. This approach considerably reduces the huge computational efforts that are normally connected to re-assessing the entire set of SC arguments.

5   SoR Example Including DMSC Integration

Fleets of autonomous transport vehicles (ATVs) are used in factories to automate transport in the production chain. A whole fleet of ATVs is an SoS that enables cooperative goal fulfilment. To operate and perform transfer orders, each ATV must be able detect and map obstacles invoking an obstacle mapping service. The output of this service is then used by the autonomous navigation service to move safely on the shop floor. The obstacle mapping service detects obstacles via object detection service using RGB-D camera, and includes them in its occupancy map. In our example, the transport robots utilize the features of SoA and SoR described in Sect. 3. They are members of the SoS and have already recognized themselves and their services by means of their SystemDiscovery components. As a matter of simplicity, the example focuses on two structurally identical robots (robot1, robot2) that are operating autonomously in the factory hall. The mechanisms of reconfiguration and DMSC evaluation are explained using the perspective of robot1.

At start of operation, the reconfiguration sequence is triggered for both robots to create an initial configuration of services that implements obstacle mapping in line with the given performance and safety goals. For this purpose, the Reconfiguration component chooses the obstacle mapping blueprint of shown in Fig. 2. This integrates a camera service blueprint, an obstacle detection service blueprint and an occupancy map service blueprint which have to be instantiated by the use of services or service compositions provided either by robot1 or robot2. Reconfiguration now is looking for consumable services using SystemDiscovery (1), which lists the available service instances that can be used for instantiating basic service blueprints and service composition blueprints. In Table 1, all services available to robot1 and their respective failure rates are shown. Note that robot2 is using older generation hardware, which reflects into the failure rates of some of the services. Further, Table 2 displays different feasible configurations (c_n) with their performance and safety properties, again taking the perspective of robot1. To keep the example simple, possible configurations are limited to c_1, c_2, c_3, and c_4. After successful creation of the set of possible configurations, reconfiguration will trigger safety evaluation.

Table 1. List of registered services as discovered by robot1

Service	System	Failure rate $\lambda_{r_n s_m}$	
RGB-D camera service	robot1	$\lambda_{r_1 s_1}$	$2.00 \cdot 10^{-5} h^{-1}$
	robot2	$\lambda_{r_2 s_1}$	$2.00 \cdot 10^{-5} h^{-1}$
Obstacle detection service	robot1	$\lambda_{r_1 s_2}$	$1.00 \cdot 10^{-5} h^{-1}$
	robot2	$\lambda_{r_2 s_2}$	$1.00 \cdot 10^{-5} h^{-1}$
Occupancy map generator service	robot1	$\lambda_{r_1 s_3}$	$1.00 \cdot 10^{-5} h^{-1}$
	robot2	$\lambda_{r_2 s_3}$	$3.00 \cdot 10^{-5} h^{-1}$
Communication channel	A	λ_A	$5.00 \cdot 10^{-5} h^{-1}$
	B	λ_B	$5.00 \cdot 10^{-5} h^{-1}$

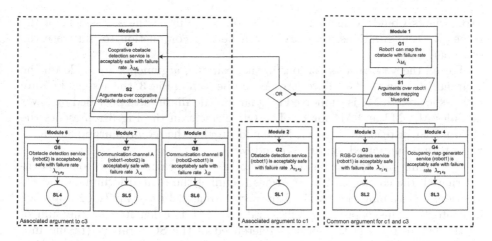

Fig. 3. Combined Safety Cases associating to c_1 and c_3

As explained in Sect. 4, the modular SC arguments are built and associated to blueprints at design-time. For simplicity, we only consider the rate of safety-critical failures as the only safety property associated to each service (we use the term "failure rate" for the remainder of this paper). The top goal G1 for the "obstacle mapping" service composition blueprint is supported by a strategy S1 associated to the service composition blueprint (see Fig. 3). This strategy references sub-goals associated to the constituting services. If the constituting services are basic services, their goals are supported by solutions (Sl_n) that are established at design-time, e.g., by Fault Tree Analysis (FTA). If the constituting services are service compositions, then again strategies are associated to them that reference sub-goals for constituting services. This is the case for configuration c_3 in Fig. 3, where instead of the SC module associated to the local robot1 obstacle detection service M5 is invoked that builds an argument for the combination of the robot2 obstacle detection service and the communication channels used to enable this remote service. In Fig. 3, we show the two variants of the SoS SC reconstructed at run-time for configurations c_1 and c_3 (actually, these

Table 2. Possible configurations $(c_1, ..., c_4)$ for robot1 and their associated safety (failure rate) and performance properties

	RGB-D camera service	Obstacle detection service	Occupancy map generator service	Failure rate λ_{M_1}	Performance (6 = best)
c_1	robot1	robot1	robot1	$4.00 \cdot 10^{-5} h^{-1}$	6
c_2	robot1	robot1	robot2	$1.60 \cdot 10^{-4} h^{-1}$	5
c_3	robot1	robot2	robot1	$1.40 \cdot 10^{-4} h^{-1}$	5
c_4	robot1	robot2	robot2	$1.60 \cdot 10^{-4} h^{-1}$	4

two variants would be reconstructed sequentially during the assessment of the respective configurations; they are shown here in conjunction to illustrate the concept).

For all the service compositions in the example, arguments are build on the guaranteed value for the failure rate. As can be seen in Fig. 3, the assumed failure rate associated to M1 is supported by guaranteed failure rates provided by lower modules M2, M3 and M4 for c_1. The OR element in the Fig. 3 represents the option, that instead of M2 in c_1, M5 could provide the required argument in c_3. S2 in turn is supported by M6, M7 and M8.

The failure rate for the higher level module M1 is calculated bottom-up considering all the connected SC strategies (defining the related formulas) and SC solutions (containing the required property values). In a simplifying approach in context of this paper, the failure rate for M1 is calculated as the sum of all the failure rates of the services referenced in the SC strategy (taking into account that the constituting services are arranged in series, and assuming that failures are independent). The result of this computation of actual values of course depends on the configuration: For configuration c_1 we integrate three services, whilst for configuration c_3 five services are involved. Thus, the actual value for M1 (λ_{M_1}) may vary for each configuration due to the structural differences between the configurations, despite the actual values for invoked basic services being constant during run-time.

$$c_1 : \lambda_{M_1} = \lambda_{r_1 s_1} + \lambda_{r_1 s_2} + \lambda_{r_1 s_3} = 4.00 \cdot 10^{-5} h^{-1} \tag{1}$$

$$c_2 : \lambda_{M_1} = \lambda_{r_1 s_1} + \lambda_{r_1 s_2} + (\lambda_A + \lambda_{r_2 s_3} + \lambda_B) = 1.60 \cdot 10^{-4} h^{-1} \tag{2}$$

$$c_3 : \lambda_{M_1} = \lambda_{r_1 s_1} + (\lambda_A + \lambda_{r_2 s_2} + \lambda_B) + \lambda_{r_1 s_3} = 1.40 \cdot 10^{-4} h^{-1} \tag{3}$$

$$c_4 : \lambda_{M_1} = \lambda_{r_1 s_1} + (\lambda_A + \lambda_{r_2 s_2} + \lambda_B) + \lambda_{r_1 s_3} = 1.60 \cdot 10^{-4} h^{-1} \tag{4}$$

The highlighted interfaces and properties are included in the contract associated to each module. During re-evaluation, the assume-guarantee dependencies within inter-module contracts are verified for each configuration. In our example, the actual values for the failure rate property is propagated from bottom to top to see if any guaranteed value in the module contracts is violated.

For c_1 all the values guaranteed by the invoked basic services fulfill the assumption embedded in the SC strategy S1. Consequently, a re-calculation of the actual value for the higher level (M1) is not necessary; c_1 is a valid configuration. For c_3 the actual failure rate for the "obstacle detection" service composition involving robot2 is higher than the actual failure rate of the original basic service of robot1, since in this service composition, also the additional failure rates of the communication channels must be considered (see Eq. 3), which is in line with SC strategy S2 in Fig. 3. Still, even this higher combined failure rate meets the goal G5 defined in the respective SC module, so the re-calculation can be stopped here and also c_3 is evaluated as a valid configuration. For c_2 and c_4, the respective safety goals for the service compositions are violated, which propagates also in a violation of the top-level safety goal G1.

For each possible configuration, the SC evaluation result is shared with the Reconfiguration component. It enables the Reconfiguration component to

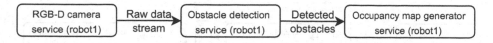

Fig. 4. Service composition of configuration c_1 using services provided by robot1

establish the set of valid configurations, which in our example contains only c_1 and c_3. For these valid configurations, the Reconfiguration component evaluates service properties with respect to performance goals as a means to select the best performing configuration. In this simplified example we assume that each individual services not provided locally but by other systems in the SoS will reduce performance. To calculate, we decided to weight services according to their origin. Thus, a service provided by the own system has a weight of 2 and a service provided by another member of the SoS has a weight of 1, and the sum of all service weights in a service composition represents the performance (such, the highest value represents the best performance). In Table 2, the individual configurations and their SC and performance evaluation results are listed. As visible there, c_1 and c_3 are valid configurations, of which c_1 has the best performance and is therefor selected. After selecting c_1, the Reconfiguration component activates all services referenced in c_1 and links their interfaces as depicted in Fig. 4.

Now robot1 will localize obstacles and integrate them into the navigation map by using the local RGB-D camera service which is connected to the local obstacle detection service, which in turn provides obstacle information to the local occupancy map generator service.

After some period of time, we assume that the hardware running the obstacle detection service of robot1 fails so that this service instance becomes unavailable. This failure affect the list of available services in SystemDiscovery and will trigger reconfiguration, again with the same set of safety and performance goals. Reconfiguration is now again using the "obstacle mapping" blueprint. Because of the unavailable obstacle detection service provided by robot1, the list of possible configuration generated by the Reconfiguration component now only contains c_3 and c_4. Once again, the SafetyEvaluation component recreates the SC for these two configurations and assesses their validity in terms of the safety goals. As in previous calculations, this shows that for c_3 the safety goals are met, and for c_4 they are violated. Therefore, the set of valid configurations this time contains only c_3 (shown in Fig. 5), which also turns out as the best performing (note that this is a drastically simplified example - in reality we will have many valid configurations entering the performance evaluation).

Reconfiguration will now stop services of c_1 if they are not needed in c_3 and will start and connect services newly integrated into c_3 (actually, for the obstacle detection service provided by robot2, robot1 needs to send a request to robot2 to start the service, similarly for some elements of the communication services). After completing reconfiguration, robot1 can continue to operate safely despite a local failure by using a service provided by another system in the SoS.

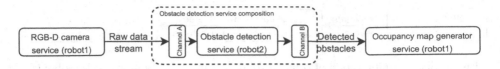

Fig. 5. Configuration c_3 instantiated with RGB-D camera service and occupancy map service provided by robot1 and obstacle detection service provided by robot2

6   Conclusion and Future Research

This paper presents the concept of Service-oriented Reconfiguration (SoR), and an extension of the SoR concept for run-time assurance of the SoS by using Dynamic Modular Safety Case (DMSC). The concepts are based on systems using a Service-oriented Architecture (SoA) which supports constructing service configurations from local and remote service instances. Blueprints provide the structural information that is used to derive all possible configurations taking into account the service instances discovered in the SoS. In the original SoR concept, the best performing configuration is selected from the set of possible configurations and implemented. This concept is now extended by a safety-related evaluation step that checks if possible configurations are valid in the sense that they fulfill predefined safety goals. The performance-oriented selection of the SoR now only takes the set of these valid configurations as an input, and selects the best performing of the valid configurations. To achieve this, design-time created modular SC information (SC solutions, strategies, and goals) are combined with an assume-guarantee-type contract scheme that allows re-constructing and assessing the SC for each configuration at run-time. Thus, SoS are now able to flexibly reconfigure at run-time using local and remote services, and are able to assure the safety of the new configurations by creating and assessing the associated SC at run-time.

Future work will aim to extend the presented concepts by supporting the triggering of reconfiguration as a result of run-time monitoring and state verification. In addition, we plan to extend the DMSC run-time capabilities by covering more complex safety-related properties and property relations in a machine-comprehensible manner. A third direction of future work is to evolve the current concept of local evaluation of performance goals into an approach shared and collaboratively executed by all SoS participants.

References

1. Zeigler, B., Mittal, S., Traoré, M.: MBSE with/out simulation: state of the art and way forward. Systems **6**, 40 (2018). https://doi.org/10.3390/systems6040040
2. Lee, E.A.: Cyber physical systems: design challenges. In: 2008 11th IEEE International Symposium on Object and Component-Oriented Real-Time Distributed Computing (ISORC), pp. 363–369, May 2008. https://doi.org/10.1109/ISORC.2008.25

3. Zhou, M., Li, H.X., Weijnen, M.: A Complex Adaptive System of Systems Approach to Human-Automation Interaction in Smart Grid, pp. 425–500. Wiley-IEEE Press (2015). https://doi.org/10.1002/9781119036821.ch12
4. Despotou, G., Alexander, R., Hall-May, M.: Key concepts and characteristics of systems of systems (2003)
5. Bradbury, J.S., Cordy, J.R., Dingel, J., Wermelinger, M.: A survey of self-management in dynamic software architecture specifications. In: Proceedings of the 1st ACM SIGSOFT Workshop on Self-Managed Systems, WOSS 2004, pp. 28–33. Association for Computing Machinery, New York (2004). https://doi.org/10.1145/1075405.1075411
6. Sinreich, D.: An architectural blueprint for autonomic computing. Technical report, IBM (2006)
7. Salehie, M., Tahvildari, L.: Towards a goal-driven approach to action selection in self-adaptive software. Softw. Pract. Exp. 42(2), 211–233 (2012). https://doi.org/10.1002/spe.1066
8. Mauro, J., Nieke, M., Seidl, C., Yu, I.C.: Context aware reconfiguration in software product lines. In: Proceedings of the Tenth International Workshop on Variability Modelling of Software-Intensive Systems, VaMoS 2016, pp. 41–48. Association for Computing Machinery, New York (2016). https://doi.org/10.1145/2866614.2866620
9. Rosa, L., Rodrigues, L., Lopes, A., Hiltunen, M., Schlichting, R.: Self-management of adaptable component-based applications. IEEE Trans. Softw. Eng. 39(3), 403–421 (2013). https://doi.org/10.1109/TSE.2012.29
10. Hu, M., Liao, Y., Wang, W., Li, G., Cheng, B., Chen, F.: Decision tree-based maneuver prediction for driver rear-end risk-avoidance behaviors in cut-in scenarios. J. Adv. Transp. 2017, 1–12 (2017)
11. Wang, F.Y.: Parallel control and management for intelligent transportation systems: concepts, architectures, and applications. IEEE Trans. Intell. Transp. Syst. 11(3), 630–638 (2010). https://doi.org/10.1109/TITS.2010.2060218
12. Ding, Z., Zhou, Y., Zhou, M.: Modeling self-adaptive software systems with learning petri nets. IEEE Trans. Syst. Man Cybern. Syst. 46(4), 483–498 (2016). https://doi.org/10.1109/TSMC.2015.2433892
13. Zeadally, S., Sanislav, T., Mois, G.D.: Self-adaptation techniques in cyber-physical systems (CPSs). IEEE Access 7, 171126–171139 (2019). https://doi.org/10.1109/ACCESS.2019.2956124
14. Kosmalska, A.: Flexilience: balancing key requirements in autonomous systems. https://safe-intelligence.fraunhofer.de/flexilience. Accessed 11 June 2021
15. Sillmann, B., Gruber, K., Glock, T., Sax, E.: Multi-objective optimization of system of systems architectures for vehicle to infrastructure applications using an evolutionary algorithm. In: 2018 IEEE International Systems Engineering Symposium (ISSE), pp. 1–5 (2018). https://doi.org/10.1109/SysEng.2018.8544390
16. Feng, X., Wäppling, D., Andersson, H., Ölvander, J., Tarkian, M.: Multi-objective optimization in industrial robotic cell design. In: DAC 2010 (2010)
17. Willigen, W.V., Haasdijk, E., Kester, L.: A multi-objective approach to evolving platooning strategies in intelligent transportation systems. In: GECCO 2013 (2013)
18. Dovgan, E., Gams, M., Filipič, B.: A real-time multiobjective optimization algorithm for discovering driving strategies. Transp. Sci. 53(3), 695–707 (2019). https://doi.org/10.1287/trsc.2018.0872

19. Schneider, E.: A middleware approach for dynamic real-time software reconfiguration on distributed embedded systems: networking and internet architecture. Ph.D. thesis, Louis Pasteur University (2004). https://tel.archives-ouvertes.fr/tel-00011926
20. Kelly, T.P.: Arguing safety, a systematic approach to managing safety cases. Ph.D. thesis, University of York, York, United Kingdom (1998)
21. Modular software safety case (MSSC) (2012). https://www.amsderisc.com/wp-content/uploads/2013/01/MSSC_101_Issue_01_PD_2012_11_17.pdf
22. Denney, E., Pai, G., Habli, I.: Dynamic safety cases for through-life safety assurance. In: Proceedings of the 37th International Conference on Software Engineering, ICSE 2015, vol. 2, pp. 587–590. IEEE Press (2015)
23. Mirzaei, E., Thomas, C., Conrad, M.: Safety cases for adaptive systems of systems: state of the art and current challenges. In: Bernardi, S., et al. (eds.) EDCC 2020. CCIS, vol. 1279, pp. 127–138. Springer, Cham (2020). https://doi.org/10.1007/978-3-030-58462-7_11
24. Goal Structuring Notation Community Standard (Version 2). The Assurance Case Working Group, PO Box 1866, Mountain View, CA 94042, USA (2018). www.scsc.uk/gc
25. Benvenuti, L., Ferrari, A., Mazzi, E., Vincentelli, A.L.S.: Contract-based design for computation and verification of a closed-loop hybrid system. In: Egerstedt, M., Mishra, B. (eds.) HSCC 2008. LNCS, vol. 4981, pp. 58–71. Springer, Heidelberg (2008). https://doi.org/10.1007/978-3-540-78929-1_5
26. Fenn, J., Hawkins, R., Williams, P., Kelly, T., Banner, M., Oakshott, Y.: The who, where, how, why and when of modular and incremental certification. In: IET Conference Proceedings, pp. 135–140(5), January 2007. https://digital-library.theiet.org/content/conferences/10.1049/cp20070454
27. Björnander, S., Land, R., Graydon, P., Lundqvist, K., Conmy, P.: A method to formally evaluate safety case arguments against a system architecture model. In: 2nd edition of the IEEE Workshop on Software Certification (WoSoCER2012). IEEE Computer Society, November 2012. http://www.es.mdh.se/publications/2687
28. Graydon, M., Bate, I.: The nature and content of safety contracts: challenges and suggestions for a way forward. In: Proceedings of IEEE Pacific Rim International Symposium on Dependable Computing, PRDC, pp. 135–144, December 2014. https://doi.org/10.1109/PRDC.2014.24
29. Bates, S., Bate, I., Hawkins, R., Kelly, T., McDermid, J., Fletcher, R.: Safety case architectures to complement a contract-based approach to designing safe systems. In: Proceedings of the 21st International System Safety Conference (ISSC) (2003)
30. Jaradat, O., Bate, I., Punnekkat, S.: Using sensitivity analysis to facilitate the maintenance of safety cases. In: de la Puente, J.A., Vardanega, T. (eds.) Ada-Europe 2015. LNCS, vol. 9111, pp. 162–176. Springer, Cham (2015). https://doi.org/10.1007/978-3-319-19584-1_11
31. Jaradat, O., Bate, I.: Deriving hierarchical safety contracts. In: 2015 IEEE 21st Pacific Rim International Symposium on Dependable Computing (PRDC), pp. 119–128 (2015). https://doi.org/10.1109/PRDC.2015.21
32. Jaradat, O.T.S., Bate, I.: Using safety contracts to guide the maintenance of systems and safety cases. In: 2017 13th European Dependable Computing Conference (EDCC), pp. 95–102 (2017). https://doi.org/10.1109/EDCC.2017.20
33. Jaradat, O., Punnekkat, S.: Using safety contracts to verify design assumptions during runtime. In: Casimiro, A., Ferreira, P.M. (eds.) Ada-Europe 2018. LNCS, vol. 10873, pp. 3–18. Springer, Cham (2018). https://doi.org/10.1007/978-3-319-92432-8_1

34. Jaradat, O., Sljivo, I., Hawkins, R., Habli, I.: Modular safety cases for the assurance of industry 4.0. In: Safety-Critical Systems Symposium, February 2020
35. Calinescu, R., Weyns, D., Gerasimou, S., Iftikhar, M.U., Habli, I., Kelly, T.: Engineering trustworthy self-adaptive software with dynamic assurance cases. IEEE Trans. Softw. Eng. **44**(11), 1039–1069 (2018). https://doi.org/10.1109/TSE.2017.2738640
36. Asaadi, E., Denney, E., Menzies, J., Pai, G.J., Petroff, D.: Dynamic assurance cases: a pathway to trusted autonomy. Computer **53**(12), 35–46 (2020). https://doi.org/10.1109/MC.2020.3022030
37. Cheng, B.H.C., Clark, R.J., Fleck, J.E., Langford, M.A., McKinley, P.K.: AC-ROS: assurance case driven adaptation for the robot operating system. In: Proceedings of the 23rd ACM/IEEE International Conference on Model Driven Engineering Languages and Systems, MODELS 2020, pp. 102–113. Association for Computing Machinery, New York (2020). https://doi.org/10.1145/3365438.3410952
38. Denney, E., Pai, G., Habli, I.: Dynamic safety cases for through-life safety assurance. In: 2015 IEEE/ACM 37th IEEE International Conference on Software Engineering, vol. 2, pp. 587–590 (2015). https://doi.org/10.1109/ICSE.2015.199
39. Denney, E., Pai, G.: Automating the assembly of aviation safety cases. IEEE Trans. Reliab. **63**(4), 830–849 (2014). https://doi.org/10.1109/TR.2014.2335995
40. Denney, E., Pai, G.: Towards a formal basis for modular safety cases. In: Koornneef, F., van Gulijk, C. (eds.) SAFECOMP 2015. LNCS, vol. 9337, pp. 328–343. Springer, Cham (2015). https://doi.org/10.1007/978-3-319-24255-2_24
41. Schneider, D., Trapp, M.: Conditional safety certification of open adaptive systems. ACM Trans. Auton. Adapt. Syst. **8**(2) (2013). https://doi.org/10.1145/2491465.2491467
42. Trapp, M., Schneider, D., Weiss, G.: Towards safety-awareness and dynamic safety management. In: 2018 14th European Dependable Computing Conference (EDCC), pp. 107–111 (2018). https://doi.org/10.1109/EDCC.2018.00027
43. Feth, P., Schneider, D., Adler, R.: A conceptual safety supervisor definition and evaluation framework for autonomous systems. In: Tonetta, S., Schoitsch, E., Bitsch, F. (eds.) SAFECOMP 2017. LNCS, vol. 10488, pp. 135–148. Springer, Cham (2017). https://doi.org/10.1007/978-3-319-66266-4_9
44. Schneider, D., Trapp, M.: B-space: dynamic management and assurance of open systems of systems. J. Internet Serv. Appl. **9**, 1–16 (2018)
45. Moncada, D.S.V., et al.: Dynamic Safety Certification for Collaborative Embedded Systems at Runtime, pp. 171–196. Springer, Cham (2021). https://doi.org/10.1007/9783030621360_8
46. Siefke, L., Sommer, V., Wudka, B., Thomas, C.: Robotic systems of systems based on a decentralized service-oriented architecture. Robotics **9**(4), 78 (2020). https://doi.org/10.3390/robotics9040078
47. Richardson, C.: Microservices Patterns: With Examples in Java, 1st edn. Manning Publications, Shelter Island, New York (2018)
48. Wudka, B., Thomas, C., Siefke, L., Sommer, V.: A reconfiguration approach for open adaptive systems-of-systems. In: 2020 IEEE International Symposium on Software Reliability Engineering Workshops (ISSREW), Los Alamitos, CA, USA, pp. 219–222. IEEE Computer Society, October 2020. https://doi.org/10.1109/ISSREW51248.2020.00076

Behavior Prediction of Cyber-Physical Systems for Dynamic Risk Assessment

Marta Grobelna[✉]

Fraunhofer IKS, Munich, Germany
marta.grobelna@iks.fraunhofer.de

Abstract. Cyber-Physical Systems, such as autonomous vehicles, have the potential for providing more safety by restricting the impact of potentially unreliable human operators. However, ensuring that the system, i.e. the CPS under consideration, will behave safely under any conditions is not straightforward. The complexity of the environment and the system itself, causes uncertainties that need to be considered by the safety measures. The challenge for an autonomous system is to find the optimal trade-off between safety and utility without human intervention. Consequently, such systems has to be self-adaptive and predictive in order to forecast hazardous situations and react to them before the happen. This paper sketches how reachability analysis in combination with game theory can be used to predict risk of hazardous situations.

Keywords: Dynamic risk assessment · Game theory · Reachability analysis · Self-adaptation

1 Introduction

According to the US National Highway Traffic Safety Administration, driver's inattention, distractions, and inadequate surveillance are the main reasons for human caused accidents on the roads [13]. This indicates that autonomous Cyber-Physical Systems (CPSs), such as autonomous vehicles (AVs), have the potential for providing more safety by restricting the impact of potentially unreliable human operators. Guaranteeing safety of such systems under any conditions is challenging as a full functional specification of the system and its environment is infeasible. First, the high complexity of the environment in which the system operates makes it impossible to consider all factors that influence its behavior. Second, it might be unknown how the factors affect the behavior of the system. For instance, the behavior of human traffic participants represent such factor as their intentions are unknown.

On account of these shortcomings, CPSs have to be *self-adaptive*. This means that such systems have to be able to detect hazards and, if necessary, calculate adequate adaptation steps to counter the hazards on time without human intervention. The self-adaptation process consists of four steps: monitor, analyze, plan, and execute. The system monitors the environment and analyzes the data

© Springer Nature Switzerland AG 2021
R. Adler et al. (Eds.): EDCC 2021 Workshops, CCIS 1462, pp. 30–38, 2021.
https://doi.org/10.1007/978-3-030-86507-8_3

to extract information needed to understand the current situation. Subsequently, if necessary, adaptation steps, such as trajectory adaptations, are planned and then executed. Since the actions of the system have an impact on the environment, and changes in the environment have an impact on the behavior of the CPS, there is a feedback loop from the execution step to the monitoring step [1].

In order to plan the adaptation steps on time, and so prevent or recover from an undesired situation, the situation has to be *predicted* [2]. This requires the estimation of future states of the system, i.e. of the CPS which safe behavior needs to be guaranteed, and other agents that are part of the system's environment, e.g. other traffic participants. For this purpose, the system has to use models that reflect the behavior of the agents at a higher level of abstraction, making the required calculations feasible during the run time. After the estimation of the future states, the risk of a hazardous situation can be quantitatively assessed. Here, risk is defined according to ISO 26262 as a 'combination of the probability of occurrence of harm and the severity of that harm' [7]. In the context of AVs, an accident is an example of a hazardous situation.

Unfortunately, the non-determinism of the environment, imprecise measurements and models cause uncertainties that might have an impact on the needed estimates and so on the decision making of the system. In order to consider the uncertainties, they need to quantified, while an optimal trade-off between safety and utility has to be taken into account. On the one hand, an over-cautious treatment of the uncertainties can cause a significant decrease of system's utility and so possibly causing threats to safety. On the other hand, the system must not be too optimistic since this might cause violations of safety requirements and hazards such as accidents [14].

In context of AVs, an important source of information will be the Vehicle-to-X (V2X) communication which will enable wireless exchange of data and information with vehicles, infrastructures, and pedestrians. Even though communication is more robust against environmental circumstances such as weather conditions, there are still issues that need to be considered while using data and information received using V2X communication.

One of the main shortcomings of communication networks is the fact that the system receiving data has to trust that the information is correct. In particular, even in the era of 6G, uncertainty provided by the sensors of the sending system will remain. Further, malfunctioning or deliberate sharing of malicious data, i.e. in case of a cyber-attack, cannot be fully excluded. Further, it has to be considered that there will be a phase where cars that are not capable to communicate via V2X will be present on the roads. Also, intentions of human drivers, pedestrians, and cyclists either cannot be exchanged via V2X. Therefore, the risk assessment function has to be predictive and dynamic, meaning that it has to consider future states of the environment and adapt to the current level of uncertainty that can vary during run time. This paper presents a sketch of an approach for dynamic risk assessment that considers the need for a trade-off between safety and utility of the system while taking into account known and potentially unknown uncertainties.

2   Behavior Prediction Under Uncertainty

Self-adaptation requires prediction of potentially hazardous events which in turn requires estimation of future state of the system and the agents in its environment. This section presents how future states can be calculated under consideration of uncertainties and interactions among agents.

Three types of uncertainties are defined [4]: aleatory, epistemic and ontological. The aleatory uncertainty concerns the randomness of a process, which is considered to be irreducible. Epistemic uncertainty concerns the discrepancy between the true behavior of a system and its model. Its impact can be reduced when more information about the system is known. The ontological uncertainty is caused by a complete ignorance of a relevant factor in the model. This work focuses on aleatory and epistemic uncertainties.

2.1   Calculating Reachable States

Systems that exhibit continuous behavior can be described in terms of differential equations. In case the system can switch between different modes of dynamics, the system is called hybrid and can be represented by a hybrid automaton where each mode of dynamics is associated with a separate location [6]. Given the model, future states of the system can be calculated using reachability analysis (RA) which is a well-known formal method to iteratively calculate reachable sets of states within a finite time horizon given an initial state. In classical model checking, RA is usually used to estimate if the system fulfills some safety properties. For this purpose, in each iteration step the algorithm estimates if the currently reachable states intersect with the set of states that do not fulfill the desired safety properties [6,12].

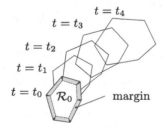

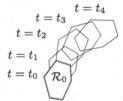

(a) Margin to compensate uncertainty.   (b) Margin for precise information.

Fig. 1. Reachability analysis output for an initial state $\mathcal{R}_0$ and the time horizon $t = [t_0, t_4]$.

Here, the RA is used to calculate the future states of the involved agents. Figure 1 illustrates an output of a RA. The initial state, denoted by $\mathcal{R}_0$, is represented by a polyhedron and in order to account for aleatory uncertainties, such as perceptual uncertainties, it is over-approximated, meaning that in each

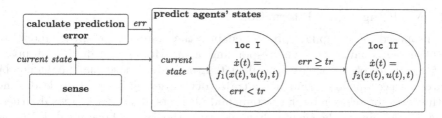

Fig. 2. Model update based on the level of trust.

dimension of the state, e.g. position or velocity, a margin is added. The successor states are then calculated by applying the dynamics to the polyhedron that is considered in current iteration step. To consider uncertainty propagation and epistemic uncertainties, in each iteration step an over-approximation is conducted. The resulting new polyhedron is then used as initial state for the next iteration of the algorithm. The system has to calculate the reachable sets of states for each agent within its environment. Based on the estimated future occupancy of the agents, it can plan its adaptation steps if necessary.

The challenge is to over-approximate the states such that on the one hand, all relevant states are considered but on the other hand, the over-approximations are not over-conservative, i.e. the added margin is not too large. In particular, this is important for finding the optimal trade-off between safety and utility of the system. The greater the over-approximations, the more cautious are the predictions, leaving the system less degrees of freedom for adaptations.

One possible way to overcome this challenge is to link the over-approximation magnitude with the prediction error, i.e. the discrepancy between the predicted and the true behavior of the particular agent. Figure 2 illustrates the idea for a single agent. By sensing, the system gains information about the current state of the other agent. Given the predicted states from the previous cycle, it can estimate the prediction error. To calculate the future states of the system, a hybrid automaton with at least two locations is needed. For instance, one location might reflect defensive behavior and the second aggressive behavior. Further, for each location a different over-approximation margin can be defined. In Fig. 2 the automaton has two locations – loc I and loc II – each having different dynamics $\dot{f}_1(x, u, t)$ and $\dot{f}_2(x, u, t)$ where x is state, u is control and t is time. As long as the invariant $err < tr$ in loc I is satisfied, i.e. when the prediction error denoted by err in Fig. 2 is lower than a certain threshold tr, the system considers loc I and is not allowed to enter loc II due to the transition guard $err \geq tr$ that prohibits the switch. The output will then look like in Fig. 1b. Otherwise, loc II where more coarse over-approximations are conducted so the output might look like in Fig. 1a. Hence, with more precise calculations the system will have more degrees of freedom for planning new trajectories.

2.2 Modeling Agent Interactions

The proposed model update process enables the system to adapt its model to the observed behavior of the corresponding agent. However, using RA all possible trajectories of the agents are calculated, including those that might not be desired by a certain agent. Further, a trajectory chosen by an agent might depend on the trajectory chosen by the system, and vice versa. In order to consider these dependencies among the agents, dynamic game theory can be applied. Dynamic games occur when a number of agents interact with each other over time while each has its own objective function [3,8].

In order to apply dynamic game theory for the estimation of future trajectories of a number of agents, several challenges need to be overcome. First, the formulated game need to deal with uncertainties regarding the objective functions of the agents. In particular, each agent might have different objectives and different preferences over multiple objectives. Both, the objectives and the priorities, might be unknown. Further, constraints such as traffic rules have to be respected, however, temporal contempt should be considered since situations might occur where agents will violate them in order to achieve a higher priority objective such as collision avoidance. Consequently, temporal relaxation of constraints should be integrated.

Another problem might be the uncertainty representation in context of reachability analysis. Recall, that the output of RA is a set of polyhedra which would be the input for the algorithm that uses the game theoretic approach.

Finally, the problem of dimensionality needs to be addressed. In order to calculate optimal strategies for multiple agents, a system of (partial) differential equations needs to be solved. Unfortunately, numerical methods suffer from the curse of dimensionality, meaning that the calculation time increases with the dimensionality of the system and so the number of considered agents. In recent years, solving high-dimensional differential equations using machine learning has received more attention. There is a number of encouraging approaches [5,9,10]. In [15] the author illustrated the effectiveness of so called Physics-Informed Neural Networks [11], however the evaluated examples were theoretical and not as complex as AVs. Thus, further research in this area is needed.

2.3 Illustrative Example

In order to illustrate the proposed approach potential and the challenges that lie ahead, a simplistic example is presented. Consider a merging scenario with two vehicles $\mathcal{V}_1$, the ego vehicle, driving on an acceleration lane and vehicle $\mathcal{V}_2$ driving on the adjacent lane which $\mathcal{V}_1$ wants to enter. A state of a vehicle $\mathcal{V}_i$, denoted by x_i where $i = \{1, 2\}$, is defined as $x_i(t) = (s_i(t), v_i(t), a_i(t))$, where t is the time, $s_i(t)$ is the position, $v_i(t)$ is the velocity. Acceleration $a_i(t)$ is a control value, and is the only parameter in the dynamics of both vehicles. In this example the initial states of the both vehicles are given by

$$x_1(0) = \left(50 \text{ m}, 27.8 \text{ m/s}, 0 \text{ m/s}^2\right) \text{ and } x_2(0) = \left(25 \text{ m}, 34.7 \text{ m/s}, 0 \text{ m/s}^2\right),$$

$$(1)$$

Table 1. Defensive dynamics for $\mathcal{V}_2$.

$\mathcal{V}_1$ \ $\mathcal{V}_2$	$a_2 = -2$	$a_2 = 0$	$a_2 = 2$
$a_1 = -2$	(-120.3, -394.3)	(-70.9, -430.3)	(-58.64, -471.5)
$a_1 = 0$	(-103.9, -354.3)	(-116.3, -390.3)	(-66.9, -431.5)
$a_1 = 2$	(-61.0, -314.3)	(-99.9, -350.3)	(-112.3, -391.5)

Table 2. Aggressive dynamics for $\mathcal{V}_2$.

$\mathcal{V}_1$ \ $\mathcal{V}_2$	$a_2 = 0$	$a_2 = 4$
$a_1 = -2$	(-70.9, -263.6)	(-52.0, 6.6)
$a_1 = 0$	(-116.3, -223.6)	(-54.6, -295.6)
$a_1 = 2$	(-99.9, -183.6)	(-62.9, -255.6)

The ego vehicle is allowed to initiate the lane change if and only if it can maintain a safe distance to $\mathcal{V}_2$. Further, it is assumed that the vehicles cannot communicate with each other. Hence, $\mathcal{V}_1$ does not know if $\mathcal{V}_2$ will let it merge in front of it.

The model used by $\mathcal{V}_1$ to predict the behavior of $\mathcal{V}_2$ consists of two locations, where in each the following well-known equations of motion are contained

$$s_i(t) = s_{i,0} + v_{i,0} \cdot t + \frac{1}{2} \cdot a_i(t) \cdot t^2, \ v_i(t) = v_{i,0} + a_i(t) \cdot t, \quad (2)$$

where $s_{i,0}$ is the initial position and $v_{i,0}$ the initial velocity. The first location reflects defensive dynamics where $\mathcal{V}_2$ respects the road speed limit of 36.1 m/s and its control value a_2 is restricted by the interval $[-2, 2]\,\mathrm{m/s^2}$. The second location reflects aggressive dynamics where $\mathcal{V}_2$ does not respect the speed limit and a_2 is within the interval $[0, 4]\,\mathrm{m/s^2}$.

It is assumed that $\mathcal{V}_1$ wants to plan its trajectory for the next 2 s. Further, for sake of simplicity, it is assumed that it has perfect information and so calculation of future states reduces to evaluation of (2). The objective function of $\mathcal{V}_\in$ is given by

$$\max \ J_2(x_1, x_2, a_1, a_2, t) = - \underbrace{(v_{\max} - v_2(t))}_{\text{maximize velocity}} - 10 \cdot \underbrace{(d_{\text{safe}} - (s_1(t) - s_2(t)))}_{\text{maximize distance}}. \quad (3)$$

The first term expresses that $\mathcal{V}_2$ wants to maximize its velocity and the second term expresses that it wants to maximize the distance to $\mathcal{V}_1$ is case it follows $\mathcal{V}_2$. The second term is scaled by factor 10 to model priority of safe distance over optimal velocity. In defensive mode d_{safe} for $\mathcal{V}_2$ is 50 m and in aggressive mode 33.3 m.

The objective of $\mathcal{V}_1$ is to minimize the time until merging so its first objective is to minimize the function obtained by solving $(s_1(t) - s_2(t))^2 = d_{\text{safe}}^2$ for t. Further, it also wants to maximize its velocity and maintain safe distance which is always 50 m.

Now, a strategic game can be formulated where $\mathcal{V}_1$ is the row player and $\mathcal{V}_2$ is the column player. The objective functions were formulated such that both need to be maximized. The goal is to calculate Nash equilibria where neither player can improve its utility by changing its strategy.

Table 1 contains the payoff matrix obtained for the game where defensive behavior of V_2 was assumed. This game has only one equilibrium that is marked blue in Table 1. As expected, V_2 will let V_1 merge in front of it, since the best output for both vehicles is achieved when V_1 accelerates while V_2 decelerates. However, the output of the game is different when V_1 has the information that V_2's initial position is at 46.84 m. In this case the game has four equilibria indicating that state uncertainty has a significant impact on the output of the game and sophisticated solution to this problem needs to be found.

In case aggressive behavior of V_2 is assumed, the payoffs contained in Table 2 are obtained. This game has again a single Nash equilibria, which shows that V_2 will accelerate and not allow V_1 to merge in front of it.

While being simplistic and only considering two vehicles with perfect information and limited choices, this illustrative example shows the potential for analysis and optimization of the proposed approach. Regarding the challenges that lie ahead, defining scalable models (several vehicles/choices), improving upon imperfect information by enabling communication to make better decisions, and modeling uncertainties (e.g., with Bayesian game models), among others, will be tackled.

3   Risk Assessment

The evaluation of the models will enable timely detection of hazardous situations. In particular, a collision is detected as soon as the set of reachable states of the system intersects with a reachable set of states of any other agent surrounding it. Due to the fact that during the computation of the reachable sets of states over-approximations are made, the criterion of intersection might be too hard. Instead, the risk of that intersection should be calculated. This is a relaxation of the intersection criterion which will avoid over-cautious behavior of the system and so improve its utility. Consequently, in each iteration step of the RA, instead of a simple intersection check the risk of that intersection is calculated.

Assume n agents ($n \in \mathbb{N}$ and $n < \infty$) in the system's environment that have to be considered. Denote the sets of states that are reachable by the n agents within a time horizon t_h by $\mathcal{R}_{\text{all}}$. Since RA is iterative, the time is discretized using a time step size of t_s. Hence, for each agent the system calculated $m := t_h/t_s$ reachable sets of states. The set that an agent $a \in \{1, \ldots, n\}$ will reach at time $t_k \in \{t_1, t_2, t_3, \ldots, t_m\}$ is denoted by $\mathcal{R}_a^{t_k}$. Then the overall risk R of an intersection is given by

$$R(\mathcal{R}_{\text{all}}) := \sum_{t=1}^{m} f_s \left(\bigcap_{a=1}^{n} \mathcal{R}_a^{t_k} \right) \cdot f_p \left(\bigcap_{a=1}^{n} \mathcal{R}_a^{t_k} \right), \tag{4}$$

where $f_s(\cdot)$ is a function that estimates the severity of an intersection, $f_p(\cdot)$ is a function that estimates the probability of that intersection. Since for the evaluation of (4), the system will always consider the current information about the agents, and the behavior model for each agent can be updated, the system estimates the risk in a dynamical way under consideration of dependencies among agents due to the game theoretic approach integrated in the RA approach.

Based on the calculated risk of each trajectory that the system might choose to proceed with, it can decide which one is the safest. A high level or risk means that the safety of the system is low, while a low level of risk means a high level of safety. Hence, risk is inversely proportional to safety. Note that the same holds for the utility of a system which can also be describe by a function. The higher the risk of a hazard, the less utility can be achieved.

4   Conclusion

This paper proposes an approach that enables CPSs to be self-adaptive and account for uncertainties while finding suitable trade-offs between safety and utility of the system. In order to plan optimal adaptation steps on time, the system has to predict its own and the environments' states. This requires models able to approximate the behavior of other agents while being computationally affordable. Besides aleatory uncertainties, epistemic uncertainties as well as agent interactions have to be considered. Combining RA with game theory will allow conducting precise predictions of hazardous situations and so enable the CPSs to react to such situations on time and potentially in a more sophisticated way.

References

1. Arcaini, P., Riccobene, E., Scandurra, P.: Modeling and analyzing MAPE-K feedback loops for self-adaptation. In: 10th International Symposium on Software Engineering for Adaptive and Self-Managing Systems (2015)
2. Calinescu, R., Ghezzi, C., Kwiatkowska, M., Mirandola, R.: Self-adaptive software needs quantitative verification at runtime. Commun. ACM **55**(9), 69–77 (2012)
3. Engwerda, J., Reddy, P.: A positioning of cooperative differential games. In: 5th Conference on Performance Evaluation Methodologies and Tools (2011)
4. Gansch, R., Adee, A.: System theoretic view on uncertainties. In: Design, Automation Test in Europe Conference Exhibition (2020)
5. Han, J., Jentzen, A., Ee, W.: Solving high-dimensional partial differential equations using deep learning. In: Proceedings of the National Academy of Sciences (2017)
6. Henzinger, T.: The theory of hybrid automata. In: Proceedings 11th Annual IEEE Symposium on Logic in Computer Science (1996)
7. International Organization for Standardization: Road vehicles – functional safety. Standard ISO 26262–1:2018, ISO (2019)
8. Jafary, B., Rabiei, E., Diaconeasa, M., Masoomi, H., Fiondella, L., Mosleh, A.: A survey on autonomous vehicles interactions with human and other vehicles. In: 14th Conference on Probabilistic Safety Assessment and Management (2018)
9. Long, Z., Lu, Y., Ma, X., Dong, B.: PDE-net: learning PDEs from data. arXiv:1710.09668 (2018)
10. Nakamura-Zimmerer, T., Gong, Q., Kang, W.: Adaptive deep learning for high-dimensional Hamilton-Jacobi-Bellman equations. arXiv:1907.05317 (2020)

11. Raissi, M., Perdikaris, P., Karniadakis, G.E.: Physics-informed neural networks: a deep learning framework for solving forward and inverse problems involving non-linear partial differential equations. J. Comput. Phys. **378**, 686 (2019)
12. Riedmaier, S., Danquah, B., Schick, B., Diermeyer, F.: Unified framework and survey for model verification, validation and uncertainty quantification. Arch. Comput. Methods Eng. **28**(4), 2655–2688 (2020)
13. Singh, S.: Critical reasons for crashes investigated in the national motor vehicle crash causation survey. Traffic Safety Facts - Crash Stats (2015)
14. Trapp, M., Schneider, D., Weiss, G.: Towards safety-awareness and dynamic safety management. In: 2018 14th European Dependable Computing Conference (2018)
15. Winkler, S.N.: A framework including artificial neural networks in modelling hybrid dynamical systems. Ph.D. thesis, TU Wien (2020)

Autonomic Service Operation for Cloud Applications: Safe Actuation and Risk Management

João Tomás[1], André Bento[1], João Soares[2], Luís Ribeiro[2], António Ferreira[2], Rita Carreira[3], Filipe Araújo[1], and Raul Barbosa[1(✉)]

[1] Department of Informatics Engineering, University of Coimbra, CISUC, Coimbra, Portugal
rbarbosa@dei.uc.pt
[2] Fiercely, Rua Pedro Nunes, C-2.28, Coimbra, Portugal
[3] Virtual Power Solutions, Coimbra, Portugal

Abstract. Cloud-native applications consist of highly specialized and decoupled services that can be deployed, scaled and managed independently. Maintaining such applications available is a complex task for operators, because software defects and other kinds of faults can be challenging to diagnose and repair to quickly resume operations. Autonomic service operation is therefore a promising approach. However, there are risks associated to guaranteeing safe autonomic actuation, which must be managed. This paper discusses the challenges identified in the context of the development of a platform for autonomic service operation and describe the software architecture of the platform. Results show mean times to detect, diagnose and repair failures in the order of tens of seconds.

1 Introduction

Cloud computing enables organizations to deploy applications over the Internet on remote data centers managed by public providers. This model allows organizations to use computing resources elastically, by starting and stopping services according to the needs of applications. However, to take advantage of this model, it is crucial for organizations to have the necessary means to deploy, scale and operate applications in order to guarantee that they are highly available.

Conceptually, achieving high availability is a matter of ensuring that applications fail infrequently or that they are recovered swiftly once a failure occurs. That is, to improve the availability of a system, one may increase the Mean Time Between Failures (MTBF) or reduce the Mean Time To Repair (MTTR). In practice, this is easier written than done. Improving the MTBF requires applications to be thoroughly verified for every new deployment, which is strongly dependent on each specific context and development team. Hence, a viable alternative is to reduce MTTR through autonomic operation, to ensure prompt detection and mitigation of failures without involving developers nor operators.

Autonomic computing promotes the development of systems and applications that are self-managed in order to fulfill high-level service objectives specified by

© Springer Nature Switzerland AG 2021
R. Adler et al. (Eds.): EDCC 2021 Workshops, CCIS 1462, pp. 39–46, 2021.
https://doi.org/10.1007/978-3-030-86507-8_4

designers [7]. It is therefore attractive to improve MTTR through the ability of applications to self-repair, thus providing high availability in spite of failures. Complex failure modes can arise in cloud systems [2] and make this a challenge.

This paper discusses the main challenges identified in the context of an effort to build a platform for operating cloud services autonomically, which is named the Autonomic Service Operation (AESOP) project. Furthermore, the paper describes the software architecture of the platform and initial experimental results. The main focus of the work is on the autonomic management of microservices [6].

We find that autonomic actuation is strongly constrained by the risks of actuation. Moreover, the risk curve is dynamic in the sense that the same actuation plan may incur more or less severe risks depending on operational circumstances. Accordingly, the paper discusses the main challenges and risks of autonomic operation, from the perspective of cloud users who have two fundamental concerns:

- *Costly unavailability* may be caused by incorrect actuations planned by the autonomic manager. There's a risk of actuating in a way such that the system ends up in a worse situation than it was, even if the actuation is performed in response to an actual failure.
- *Unexpected expenses* may arise in the context of the pay-as-you-go pricing model used in cloud computing. There's a risk of increasing costs without control if actuations enable high resource usage, in response to events.

These concerns are inherently related to the risks of autonomic actuation. It is therefore crucial to address the safety of autonomic actuations and to dynamically manage the risks of actuation. The word *safety* is used sparsely in the context of cloud applications but one may identify critical scenarios such as Electronic Health Records (EHRs) that must be available to doctors when making crucial decisions, along with mission- and business-critical scenarios.

2   Challenges of Autonomic Service Operation

Autonomic computing [7] aims to develop systems and applications that have self-management abilities, can adapt and actuate without direct intervention from operators and developers to fulfill service level objectives (SLOs) specified by designers. Autonomy is architecturally supported by a control loop with four stages: monitor, analyze, plan and execute (MAPE).

Monitoring is conceptually simple: sensors or probes measure/collect information about the system and feed it into the control loop. A detailed design requires specific attributes to be collected, including execution traces and low-level metrics like latency, throughput, processor and memory usage. Hence, building a big picture of the system status raises several open challenges.

- *Unavailability measurement is indirect and inaccurate.* Even the most advanced tools presently used focus on HTTP errors, aiming to measure whether the total count is below the error budget. However, observability must be far more precise than counting errors to monitor cloud services adequately.

- *Measuring recovery times is disregarded in favor of best-effort.* Once a failure or anomaly occurs and recovery actions are taken, it is necessary to monitor the recovery time. Specifically, it is the time needed for resuming operations that needs focus. Nevertheless, best-effort is the current state-of-practice.
- *There's a gap between low-level metrics and high-level SLOs.* There aren't off-the-shelf sensors available for software, so applying control theory becomes difficult. Memory, CPU and network are commonly monitored but those hardly provide a good picture of whether the system is fulfilling the SLOs.
- *There's a lack of architectural knowledge.* In spite of decades of software architecture research, the scope of application is very narrow. It's well known in theory how to represent components, connectors, constraints, properties and systems, but in practice this isn't exploited for managing cloud applications.

Analysis is the second stage of the MAPE loop, aiming to identify discrepancies between the *current* state and the *desired* state. Clearly, correct analysis is fundamental for autonomic actuation, although it has its challenges.

- *There's a lack of clear contracts among services.* Once a failure is detected, the system must find the culprit component and attempt recovery. However, design by contract is not widely adopted and it is unfeasible to know if the fault was on the caller side or on the callee side.
- *Reliability of diagnosis influences the correctness of actuation.* Unless the root cause(s) of failures is reliable, actuation may take place on the basis of wrong diagnosis information.
- *The actuation risk varies according to the foreseen downtime cost.* Being roughly correct is better than precisely wrong. If the system is able to actuate with low impact then imperfect diagnosis may be fine.
- *Not all components are equally valuable.* State-of-the-art approaches focus on error counts, as a proxy to estimate unavailability. However, the foreseen downtime cost is far more important. Some components serve requests more valuable than others. This should be represented in software architectures.

Planning is the stage that determines the actuations that must take place to lead the system back to the desired state once it has deviated from it. As such, it is the stage that precedes *execution*. Therefore, the challenges of correctly planning actuations have a big impact on the actions that take place.

- *There's a need to dynamically adjust the risk of actuation.* Not all downtime has the same cost. There may be few requests coming in at a given time and the types of requests that are arriving might be non-critical. Hence, the planning stage should self-adjust to the *current* risk level.
- *It is necessary to predict the downtime generated by actuation.* Repairing and actuating over a system in operation may, inadvertently, lead to profit loss and/or incurring costs. Foreseeing such losses/costs is one of the keys to dynamic risk management. Effectively, actuation is safer when unavailability is acceptable even under the worst-case impact of self-managed actions.

– *Cloud applications should be designed for recovery.* Components should be
designed to be restartable and relocatable, with the application state being
transactionally stored in a database, and requests should be made idempotent
if feasible to simplify retries. Subsequently, the estimated loss of profit or
expenses incurred should guide the planning stage – actuation is safe when
the worst-case foreseen downtime cost falls below the service-level objectives.

   In summary, safely actuating in an autonomous manner depends on multiple
factors, including the actuation risk due to the possibility of making matters
worse. The autonomic architecture proposed aims to address these challenges.

3   Autonomic Service Operations Architecture

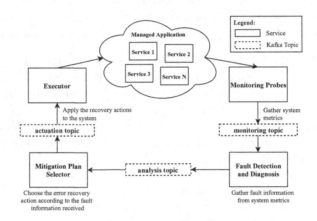

Fig. 1. Autonomic architecture overview.

Figure 1 provides an overview of the proposed architecture, which consists of four
components in the MAPE-K loop. These components take advantage of Apache
Kafka [1] as their middleware to stream messages among each other allowing the
exchange of high volume data in a fast and reliable manner.

   Regarding the loop's workflow, the managed application is observed by the
Monitoring Probes. These probes are in charge of collecting monitoring data
such as metrics, service logs, and spans from distributed tracing, and send them
to the *monitoring topic.* This data is crucial for the *Fault Detection and Diagnosis* component to detect and diagnose any possible failures. An information
record is composed whenever such anomalies are detected. The result is further
published to the *analysis topic,* to be consumed by the *Mitigation Plan Selector.*
This component, which enacts the *Planning* entity, chooses the recovery action
to be applied to the managed application. Lastly, *Knowledge* gathers the different knowledge sources that support the operation of the feedback loop, which
includes repositories where the data collected by the monitoring probes is stored.

We consider two recovery actions: 1) *restart*, which reboots the affected components; and 2) *version downgrade*, which changes the current service version to the previous one. The former action is widely used in the industry and proven to be effective in recovering failed components [4,8,9]. Furthermore, the majority of incidents in cloud systems are due to software updates (16%, according to [4]). Despite the extensive local tests that developers execute in their local environments before pushing code to production, some failures only manifest in production [4], praising the version downgrade as a recovery action.

The chosen recovery action and the name of the affected components are put together in a mitigation plan, which is sent to the *action topic*. Lastly, the *Executor* collects the recovery information to assess which components need to be recovered and communicates, for instance, with a container orchestrator to execute the required actions.

This MAPE-K loop implementation helps complement the self-healing capabilities already provided by the container orchestrator. Florio *et al.* [3] propose an implementation using a multiagent system, where each agent implements the MAPE loop and exchange information in order to make decisions. This approach can successfully scale containers, but is limited to this recovery action.

4   Implementation

To evaluate the performance of the proposed approach, we built an initial prototype (Fig. 2). The managed application is *Stan's Robot Shop* [5], an open-source microservices application with 12 microservices, written in different programming languages, which mimics an e-commerce application that sells robots.

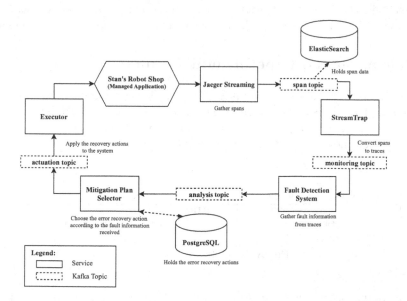

Fig. 2. Architecture implementation.

We deployed *Stan's Robot Shop* in a *Kubernetes* cluster with *Istio* service mesh, alongside the remaining architecture components. This *service mesh* uses a sidecar pattern, which attaches a proxy sidecar to each microservice. The *Envoy* proxy helps instrument the application requests with the required headers to enable distributed tracing. The sidecar then sends the required tracing information to *Jaeger*, which serves as tracing backend. The component from the tracing backend that collects spans is the *Jaeger Collector*, which then publishes them to a *Kafka* topic (effectively using the pub-sub communication paradigm).

To enable the feedback loop, we take advantage of *Jaeger Streaming* deployment strategy, which uses *Kafka* as an intermediate buffer before persisting spans to the backend storage. Since *Kafka* is the message-oriented middleware, two components collect data from the topic that holds spans - *Jaeger Ingester*, which stores spans in *Elasticsearch*, and *StreamTrap*. The latter is in charge of reconstructing traces from batches of raw spans, between 35 and 70 spans. This amount of spans provides a trade-off between the waiting time required to batch data and having enough information to reconstruct traces.

Traces are further published to the *monitoring topic*, from where they are consumed by the *Fault Detection System*. This component analyses traces and searches for Hypertext Transfer Protocol (HTTP) status codes in the range 400 (client errors) and 500 (server error). If an error is found, a record is created and sent to the *analysis topic*. This record contains the faulty components, the occurrence and detection timestamp, the protocol and the fault description.

Moreover, the *Mitigation Plan Selector* consumes records and chooses a recovery action from the database, to compose a mitigation plan. This plan contains the recovery action and the components that need to be recovered. Then, the plan is published to the *actuation topic* to be collected by the last component in the loop, the *Executor*. This component communicates with the *Kubernetes API* server to apply the recovery actions to the faulty components.

5   Validation and Experimental Results

We collected results aiming to evaluate: 1) Mean Time To Detect (MTTD), the time required to detect and diagnose faults in the managed application, and 2) MTTR, the time to repair them and bring the system to a correct service. Figure 3 depicts how these fit into the context of availability metrics.

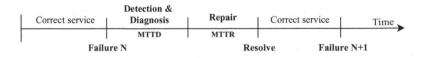

Fig. 3. Availability metrics.

The evaluation method encompasses a fault injection campaign with 100 runs. A golden run is conducted prior to the faulty runs to evaluate the system's normal state. The faulty run is composed by the three steps that follow. The *warmup* period is the first 10 s of each run and its purpose is to stabilize the system. *Peak* phase takes 90 s, excluding maintenance operations, and is the only moment when faults can be injected. The *cooldown* period takes place in the last 20 s of each run and it allows the fault to propagate in the system and become a failure. The *workload* is the load generator provided by *Stan's Robot Shop* application. Regarding *fault injection*, an exit statement is placed in the source code of the payment service to simulate a crash failure. To test the restart action, the fault is triggered periodically to emulate a *latent failure*. For the version downgrade, the fault is injected at the start of the experiment, but the faulty image is kept throughout the run to emulate a *persistent failure* that could be caused by a software update. Only one action is considered per run.

The experimental testbed is a virtual private cloud deployed on *OpenStack* with 5 virtual machines. We deployed *Kubernetes* on 4 of them with a single master and three worker nodes. The remaining machine hosts the *Elasticsearch* database, where the *Jaeger Ingester* stores spans. Each machine in the *Kubernetes* cluster has 8vCPUs, 16 GB of RAM, 100 GB of storage and runs *Debian 10*, with the exception of the database, which has 4vCPUs and 8 GB of RAM.

Figure 4 shows the experimental results. Starting by the detection time, the framework can achieve a MTTD of 4 s. However, we must consider the existing overhead from batching spans to reconstruct traces. Thus, the MTTD can further be decreased if spans are directly streamed to the *Fault Detection System*. Regarding the MTTR, there is a noticeable difference in the time that each recovery action requires. Restart takes an average of 8 s and version downgrade takes an average of 10 s. This discrepancy occurs because the version downgrade action starts by checking if any previous deployment version exists, before changing the current container image to the previous one. Furthermore, the MTTR can also be improved by using faster hardware.

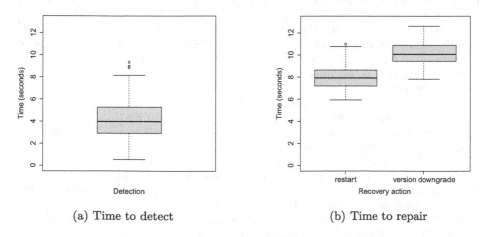

(a) Time to detect   (b) Time to repair

Fig. 4. Experimental results.

These results show the ability of the proposed solution to apply autonomic recovery actions to the system, to improve its availability. Compared to Florio *et al.* [3], our framework runs the autonomic loop continuously, while their solution runs periodically. Compared to Wu *et al.* [9], their results show a slightly higher repair time, but their solution additionally selects appropriate recovery actions.

6   Conclusion

Autonomic operation of cloud applications is an attractive approach to manage complex architectures and fulfill service objectives while reducing human intervention. However, there are risks associated to autonomic actuation, namely to cause unintended downtime and to incur unexpected expenses due to incorrect actions. This paper describes the architecture and implementation details of a platform for autonomic recovery. The results show mean times to detect, diagnose and repair in the order of tens of seconds. Hence, the results are promising because fast recovery is one of the main ways to achieve high availability.

Future directions include the development of a mechanism to select the most adequate recovery strategy, possibly including multiple actions, the measurement of whether such actuation successfully resumes operations and to attempt different recovery strategies if previous ones are deemed to be ineffective.

Acknowledgements. This work has been funded through the FCT - Foundation for Science and Technology, I.P., within the scope of project CISUC - UID/CEC/00326/2020, by the European Social Fund, through the Regional Operational Program Centro 2020, and by the AESOP project (P2020-31/SI/2017, No. 040004).

References

1. Apache Software Foundation: Apache Kafka. https://kafka.apache.org/. Accessed 01 June 2021
2. Cerveira, F., Barbosa, R., Madeira, H., Araújo, F.: The effects of soft errors and mitigation strategies for virtualization servers. IEEE Trans. Cloud Comput. (2020)
3. Florio, L., Nitto, E.D.: GRU: an approach to introduce decentralized autonomic behavior in microservices architectures (2016). https://doi.org/10.1109/ICAC.2016.25
4. Gunawi, H.S., et al.: Why does the cloud stop computing? lessons from hundreds of service outages (2016). https://doi.org/10.1145/2987550.2987583
5. Instana: Stan's robot shop, a sample microservice application (2021). https://github.com/instana/robot-shop
6. Jamshidi, P., Pahl, C., Mendonça, N.C., Lewis, J., Tilkov, S.: Microservices: the journey so far and challenges ahead. IEEE Softw. **35**(3), 24–35 (2018)
7. Kephart, J.O., Chess, D.M.: The vision of autonomic computing. Computer **36**, 41–50 (2003). https://doi.org/10.1109/MC.2003.1160055
8. Liu, H., Lu, S., Musuvathi, M., Nath, S.: What bugs cause production cloud incidents? (2019). https://doi.org/10.1145/3317550.3321438
9. Wu, L., Tordsson, J., Acker, A., Kao, O.: MicroRAS: Automatic recovery in the absence of historical failure data for microservice systems (2020)

Workshop on Dependable SOlutions for Intelligent Electricity Distribution GRIds (DSOGRI)

DSOGRI - Workshop on Dependable Solutions for Intelligent Electricity Distribution Grid

Workshop Description

Electrical distribution grids are required to deliver an increasingly more efficient and reliable supply of electricity to customers while supporting also a higher penetration of renewable energy resources. This increased penetration of renewable energy resources as well as novel prosumers like electric vehicles represent challenges for the reliability of the grid. On the other hand, the increase of available digital data through measurement devices in the grid and at customer connections (Smart Meters and grid connected inverters) facilitates novel planning and operation processes. For this purpose, Distribution System Operators (DSOs) need to implement intelligent solutions capable of guaranteeing a high level of resilience to their systems by offering new functionalities, e.g., fast identification, localization, and diagnosis of grid anomalies and faults. These functionalities allow a more effective and successful management of electricity distribution, however, they also introduce a level of interdependence between the ICT infrastructure and the electricity grid, as well as potential cyber-security vulnerabilities.

The purpose of this workshop is to investigate aspects related to the ICT-based management of failures, including cyber-security aspects, the ability to quantify the quality of the data collected from the measurement and actuation sub-systems deployed in the field, in order to make an appropriate diagnosis and detection. Moreover, the workshop provides a forum for researchers and engineers in academia and industry for discussing and analyzing current solutions and approaches, research results, experiences, and products in the field of dependable intelligent electricity grids. The ultimate goal is to present the advancement on the state of art in this domain and facilitating the adoption of resilience solutions by the distribution system operators.

The different areas or research interest include, but are not limited to:

- Dependable ICT solutions for intelligent electricity distribution grids
- ICT assisted grid fault management (detection, localization, diagnosis)
- ICT faults and their impact on grid operation
- Quantifications of data quality and of the impact of data inaccuracies on applications
- Security Threats and vulnerabilities management for digital distribution grid operation and planning
- Smart grid cyber security challenges
- Fault, attack and anomaly detection in electricity distribution grids
- Interdependencies between ICT and Electrical grid infrastructures

The 3rd edition of DSOGRI workshop is co-located with the 17th European Dependable Computing Conference (EDCC 2021). We would like to thank the Organizing Committee of EDCC 2021 for giving us the opportunity to organize the workshop and, in particular, the Workshops Chair and the Publication Chair for their support. We would also like to thank the Workshop Program Committee for the important work and support in the review phase of the papers. Last but not least, we thank all the Authors of submitted papers, hoping that DSOGRI 2021 will act as a stimulus to continue their research activities in this field.

An ICT System to Assist Earth Fault Localization

Christine Schäler[1]([⊠]), Serge Foko Fotso[1]([⊠]), Domagoj Drenjanac[1]([⊠]),
Juan Felipe Chaves[2]([⊠]), and Markus Duchon[2]([⊠])

[1] GridData GmbH, Maximilianstrasse 33, 83278 Traunstein, Germany
{schaeler,fotso,drenjanac}@griddata.eu
[2] Fortiss GmbH, Guerickestr. 25, 80805 Munich, Germany
{chaves,duchon}@fortiss.org

Abstract. Earth faults are hard to locate, but prominent failures in medium voltage electrical grids. However, to localize them in short time is essential to prevent total grid failures. There are different approaches to detect these faults, and also to determine or limit their geographical positions, in order to enable a quick elimination of the cause and thus to restore a stable network condition. To this end, an ICT system assisting fast localization is needed. Developing such an ICT system is challenging, as one needs to connect heterogeneous data and algorithmic sub-systems, scalability and low communication latency. In this paper, we propose a scalable service-oriented software architecture featuring these challenges. The architecture consists of (1) a so-called data fusion hub serving as connecting point of all sub-systems, (2) the earth fault application that localizes the faults based on signature comparison, and (3) a Message Queuing Telemetry Transport message bus for low-latency communication. Simulations are used to determine the electrical characteristics in the form of signatures to possible fault locations. Measurements of real earth faults are then compared with the simulated data to draw conclusions about the position of the fault. Once an earth fault is detected by the distribution system operator, the system calculates the probable fault locations based on the measured values and visualizes the results in the operator's network topology. In the evaluation, we show that the proposed system provides a scalable and robust solution to address the challenges of fast localization and visualization.

Keywords: Fault localization · Electricity distribution grids · Simulation · ICT architecture

1 Introduction

1.1 Motivation

An earth fault is a connection of the power circuit with the earth by accident. Earth faults are one of the most prominent case of failure in medium voltage distribution grids. To compensate them, one uses Petersen coils. However, compensating them presumes that one knows the location of the fault. To prevent a total failure of the grid, localization

© Springer Nature Switzerland AG 2021
R. Adler et al. (Eds.): EDCC 2021 Workshops, CCIS 1462, pp. 51–64, 2021.
https://doi.org/10.1007/978-3-030-86507-8_5

and compensation must happen as fast as possible. Currently, distribution grid operators (DSO) detect an earth fault by inspecting the residual current. Upon detection, to localize the fault, they try to restrict the possible locations by analyzing switching sequences and afterwards tour the possible fault locations. This approach is, however, time-consuming. To accelerate this detection by automatization, one can rely on the measurement data-driven methods that are based on signature comparisons [1]. With this method, first, in an offline step, one generates signatures based on topology data. Second, in the online phase, then compares transient measurements with these signatures. The distance from signatures to transient measurement results in probabilities for earth faults. This method has high potential to accelerate earth fault detection but is only useful if integrated into a system that can be used by the DSO. So far, such a system does not exist. Consequently, in this paper, we aim at an ICT system to assist fast localization of earth faults.

1.2 Challenges

Developing such a system imposes three challenges: (1) connecting heterogeneous sub-systems, (2) scalability and (3) low communication latency. First, one needs to connect heterogeneous sub-systems. As the signature-based method is based on grid topology and transient measurement data, one needs to connect (a) GIS systems and (b) measurement sensors providing data in various formats with the desired ICT system. These data sources need to be connected with (c) the sub-system for signature generation and (d) distance determination. Second, scalability is needed with respect to the number of measurement sensors and complexity of the grid topology, as well as with respect to the time-consuming generation of signature generation. Third, low communication latency is needed to prevent total grid failures. Consequently, one needs to rely on fast communication protocols and data storages for topology and measurement data, as well as the generated signatures, that allow to retrieve them very fast up-on distance determination. Lastly, upon detection of an earth fault, the DSO needs to be notified fast.

1.3 Contributions

In this paper we propose a scalable service-oriented software architecture assisting fast earth fault localization. It consists of three components: the data fusion hub, earth fault application, and the MQTT message bus. The data fusion hub connects heterogenous sub-systems, like headends for measurements and grid topology, with the earth fault application. In particular, it manages the signatures calculated and processed by the earth fault application. The data fusion hub supports scalability, as it features general interfaces such that an arbitrary number of measurement and topology headends can connect. The earth fault application localizes earth faults by pre-calculating signatures based on topology data in an offline phase, and then performs localization based on comparing signatures with measurement data in the online phase. The MQTT message bus ensures low communication latency between the data fusion hub and the earth fault application. In the evaluation, we show that the MQTT protocol is applicable and scalable in our architecture and the defined information flows and data transfer enables the generation of signatures as well as the comparison between these and actual earth fault measurements up to the visualization of possible fault locations.

2 Related Work

In this section, we discuss related work. To this end, we first focus on ICT architectures for topology and measurement data. Second, we focus on fault detection approaches.

2.1 ICT Architectures

A distribution system operator (DSO) typically stores different type of data in different systems. Grid topology data is typically stored in a geographic information system (GIS) [2]. They store user data about grid elements, like cable types, together with geographic information about the locations. Respective examples are ArcGIS[1] or SmallWorld[2]. However, the schema of data stored in GIS systems is not standardized making it challenging to extract all information needed for signature generation. It is not even clear whether all necessary information is contained. Additionally, GIS systems do not link grid topology data with measurements which is needed for signature comparison. In addition, there exist many systems to collect and analyze measurement data, like [3]. Most DSOs process measurements from different types of devices with different systems and for different purposes: smart meter measurement data is stored in a meter data management system, transfer point measurements and corresponding alarms in the control systems. However, all of them have in common that they do not link measurement data to the grid topology. To connect all these heterogeneous data sources, there exists the data fusion hub [4, 5] developed in the Net2DG project[3], that brings together heterogeneous data sources and data analysis sub-systems. However, the data fusion hub is currently designed for low-voltage grids and does not support signature generation and comparison in medium voltage grids. Orthogonal work focuses on data privacy and security when handling smart meter measurement data [6, 7].

2.2 Fault Detection

In addition, fault diagnosis and fault localization are the topic of a large number of already completed and still ongoing projects. Many projects focus on grid stability and deal with monitoring functionality to collect the relevant data. In general, fault detection is done in a relatively complex way, with numerous sensors (e.g., ASTROSE[4], ISOSTROSE [5]) that need to be installed in the field on the distribution grid infrastructure. Others are concerned with the development of new sensor technology that actively intervenes in the power grid (e.g., KNOPE [6]) or that requires new infrastructure (Monalisa[5]). Alternatives for monitoring the infrastructure and possibly locating faults based on temperature or communication quality have also been addressed (iMONET [7], probes in the grid).

In addition to the research activities, there are some commercial providers based on different methods. However, the term 'localization' is often used here for the detection

---

[1] https://www.arcgis.com/.

[2] https://www.mettenmeier.de/produkte-loesungen/smallworld-gis/.

[3] http://www.net2dg.eu.

[4] https://www.astrose.de/.

[5] https://www.sichere-stromnetze-durch-monitoring.de/.

and not for the localization of a fault or ground fault. With TRENCH Group[6] ground fault detection, only saturated ground faults can be localized. In NSE AG[7], for example, the direction of the earth fault can be detected using wattmetric direction detection. A method based on harmonics, comparable to the "NetzHarmonie" project [8], is offered by A. Eberle GmbH & Co. KG[8]. In addition, ROTEC Austria Vertriebsgesellschaft für Elektrotechnik GmbH[9] offers a product that combines the different methods, whereas Megger GmbH[10] also offers mobile devices.

3 Architecture Overview

In this section, we present the architecture of our proposed ICT system assisting earth fault localization. First, we provide and introduction of our system giving an overview of the general process of earth fault localization and the resulting proposed ICT architecture. Second, we present the main components of our architecture, which are the data fusion hub (DFH), MQTT message bus, and the earth fault application.

3.1 Earth Fault Detection Process and System Design

The general process of the earth fault detection system is divided into an online and an offline phase.

At first, topologies of the relevant grids need to be imported within the offline phase. On basis of the topology information and details provided by the distribution system operator a topology model or digital representation of the real grid is created. Into this model, possible fault locations are added as nodes. These fault locations are used to simulate an earth-fault event at the known position in the grid topology. Due to the modelling of the physical behavior of the grid, so called voltage and current signatures can be generated for every fault location added using different parametrizations, i.e., different resistance values. The signatures obtained by simulation with a known fault location or node identifier respectively are stored as timeseries data in a signature database for comparison later on.

According to the basic idea, each fault measurement can be mapped to a specific physical location after comparison with the simulated signature. Therefore, a distance metric was developed. In the online-phase real fault measurements are monitored by the distribution system operator's (DSO) equipment. The measured value is transferred to the application as time series data, and a distance metric is applied to identify the geographically closest signatures in comparison to the real measurement. The resulting locations that led to closest signatures in the list of possible earth-fault locations are highlighted in the topology visualization.

The overall system architecture is illustrated in Fig. 1, which connects the Data Fusion Hub (DFH) and the Earth Fault Application (EFA) for generation and comparison. For

---

[6] https://trench-group.com/.

[7] https://www.nse.ch/.

[8] https://www.a-eberle.de/.

[9] https://www.rotec-gmbh.at/.

[10] https://de.megger.com/.

the messages, we decided to use the Message Queuing Telemetry Transport (MQTT) protocol [9] established in the industry. These main components will be described in the following.

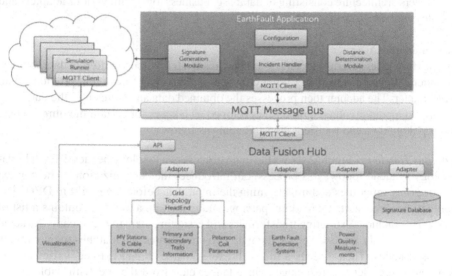

Fig. 1. Overall system architecture.

3.2 Message Queuing Telemetry Transport (MQTT)

The MQTT protocol is a standard protocol for the Internet of Things. It is a fast and lightweight protocol. In the proposed system, it is used for communication between Data Fusion Hub (see Sect. 3.3) and Earth Fault Application (see Sect. 3.4). In the remainder, we describe the topics and data transfer objects (DTOs) used. For every grid we use a set of four topics, namely ALARMS, MEASUREMENTS, SIGNATURES and FAULTLOCATIONS.

ALARMS is used to publish the occurrence of an earth fault. Within the MEASURE-MENTS topic detailed information about the measurement monitored by the DSO and time is exchanged. The SIGNATURES topic is used to exchange the simulated signatures, or to trigger the generation of new signatures for a specific topology. And the resulting, likelihood, fault locations are published on FAULT LOCATIONS.

The DTOs are implemented as Java objects and published as JSON Strings. These objects contain, among other things, information such as message type, timestamp, grid topology ID, main feeder ID, and possibly also measurement series or signatures or fault node ID and an according correlation value. By this we allow for easy expandability, interoperability and flexibility.

3.3 Data Fusion Hub (DFH)

The Data Fusion Hub connects an arbitrary number of geographic information systems (GIS) and measurement sensor with the Earth Fault Application. It follows a classical three-layers architecture consisting of database, business logic with various adapters and modules and visualization layer as follows.

Headends and Adapter
The DFH provides several adapters to connect headends tailored to different data sources. A headend processes raw data from a GIS or a measurement sensor and provides them to an adapter. The adapter then processes the obtained data and stores it in the database. To support medium voltage grids, we developed an adapter for certain medium-voltage grid topology data and transient measurements as follows.

Topology Headend. Figure 2 shows the main process of a topology headend. Each DFH-topology headend follows this process, but introduces the customization in the context of processing input files and transforming the input data before loading it in DFH. The topology headend starts by reading, parsing, and extracting a file that contains a list of nodes. This includes extracting transformers and assigning them to the already extracted nodes. Afterwards, it processes the file with geo coordinates and matches them with the processed nodes. Then it reads a file with cables, parses it and extracts various cable parameters, e.g., length, reactance, capacitance, etc., from the file with cable types. Finally, each cable entry is processed in a way that it can be uniquely identified with two already processed nodes it connects to. Furthermore, after the input data is processed and stored in the internal, in-memory, data structures, there is a module that reads these data and builds Json objects out of them. Those Json objects are converted in the set of messages which conform to the established message exchange protocol. Finally, when messages conform to the specified format, they are pushed over Web Socket connection to the DFH topology adapter which further processes them and persists in the DB.

Fig. 2. Topology headend main process.

Measurement Headend. Although there are different systems for providing measurement data, in particular, different types and format of files that contain measurements, the headend design and implementation conforms to the workflow illustrated in Fig. 3. It shows how the measurements are extracted from the input files after which they are transformed and converted to internal, in-memory, objects that hold both metadata as well as measurements data.

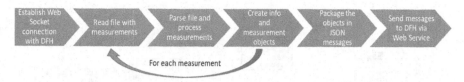

Fig. 3. Measurement headend main process.

Similar to the topology headend, after the input data is processed and stored in the internal, in-memory, data structures, there is a module that reads these data and builds Json objects out of them. Those Json objects are converted in the set of messages which conform to the established message exchange protocol. Finally, when messages conform to the specified format, they are pushed over Web Socket connection to the DFH which further processes them and persists in the DB.

In contrast to the other measurement headends, the main challenge in the current headend was how to appropriately and correctly handle measurements with microsecond resolution. The challenge was present not only on the headend side, but also on the DFH since it has to persist the measurements with the same resolution. To achieve for that, column definition in DB, that describes timestamp, had to be adapted to accommodate for such high resolution and also a special attention had to be devoted to processing timestamps. Due to the increased amount of data DFH had to be able to scale accordingly and process the data without losses. This was mainly addressed by persisting data in batches instead of persisting it message by message.

Database

The DFH connects to a MySQL database server for storing topology and measurement data as well as signatures. The respective data model is illustrated in Fig. 4. For storing topology data, there are in essence tables *GridNode* and *GridCable*. Observe that due to the split in online and offline phase (see Sect. 3.1), not all grid parameters needed for signature generations are stored in the database, but only the ones needed for storing and retrieving measurements and signatures, as well as for visualization. For storing the measurements needed in the distance determination module and connecting them to the grid topology data, the database features tables *Measurement*, *Voltage* and *Current* as shown in Fig. 5 For storing signatures, the database features the table *Signature* containing meta information of the signatures, like cable id, node id and faulty phase, as well as references to the grid and fault factors. The transient measurements have references to the signatures they belong to. A specific module in the DFH is responsible to store and retrieve signatures that relate to a specific feeder.

Visualization

To notify the DSO up-on an earth fault, the system relies on a webapplication based visualization of the fault, as shown in Fig. 6. The webapplication shows the grid topology on a map. The webapplication subscribes to the MQTT FAULLOCATIONS topic.

As long as the grid is in normal state, all nodes are green. As soon as the EFA publishes a message containing possible fault locations (see Sect. 3.4) a notification message appears on the screen and an update for the GUI is triggered. As a consequence,

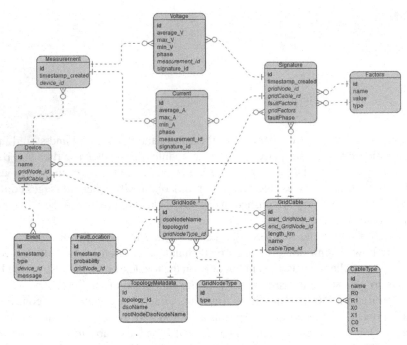

Fig. 4. Data model of the data fusion hub for storing topology, measurement, and signature data.

	measurement_Id	device_Id	headend_Id	intervalEnd	intervalStart
▶	2919	0001014E	EDAFMEHE	2019-07-30 18:13:49.377310	2019-07-30 18:13:49.377300
	2915	0001014E	EDAFMEHE	2019-07-30 18:13:49.377290	2019-07-30 18:13:49.377280
	2913	0001014E	EDAFMEHE	2019-07-30 18:13:49.377280	2019-07-30 18:13:49.377270
	2921	0001014E	EDAFMEHE	2019-07-30 18:13:49.377320	2019-07-30 18:13:49.377310
	2917	0001014E	EDAFMEHE	2019-07-30 18:13:49.377300	2019-07-30 18:13:49.377290
	2923	0001014E	EDAFMEHE	2019-07-30 18:13:49.377330	2019-07-30 18:13:49.377320
	2895	0001014E	EDAFMEHE	2019-07-30 18:13:49.377190	2019-07-30 18:13:49.377180
	2901	0001014E	EDAFMEHE	2019-07-30 18:13:49.377220	2019-07-30 18:13:49.377210
	2909	0001014E	EDAFMEHE	2019-07-30 18:13:49.377260	2019-07-30 18:13:49.377250
	2899	0001014E	EDAFMEHE	2019-07-30 18:13:49.377210	2019-07-30 18:13:49.377200

Fig. 5. Storing transient measurements in the database – excerpt of table *Measurement*.

up to three (number can be defined by configuration) nodes change their color based on the correlation value that a fault happened at the respective node. The node with the highest correlation has red color and the node with the second highest correlation has orange color. As soon as the DSO repaired a fault, the webapplication offers the functionality to reset the fault locations and colors all nodes according to the normal state, i.e., clear the local storage of the webapplication.

3.4 Earth Fault Application (EFA)

Since the application is designed to be used by different DSOs, also different deployment options are feasible. Either the EFA can be deployed on the DSOs infrastructure, on the same instance as the DFH, or at some other remote location.

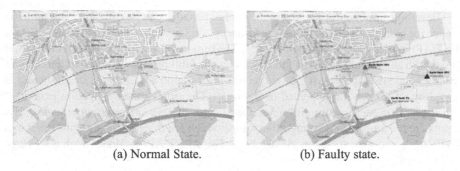

(a) Normal State.   (b) Faulty state.

Fig. 6. Visualization of an Earth fault in the GUI.

The EFA subscribes to the MQTT broker via the *Incident Handler* as a central component according to the DSOs identifier. Here, all subscriptions are handled and further processed including type checking and error handling or passed to according subcomponents. These are the *Signature Generation* and *Distance Determination* and their functionality will be explained in the following.

Figure 7 illustrates the process flow for the Signature Generation during the offline phase by the GENERATESIGNATURES DTO. The object provides among others information about the nodes and resistances to be used for the simulation. The Signature Generation component takes care of the scheduling according to the number of available docker instances. Each docker executes a single simulation run for one possible fault location and one resistance value. Once, the simulation is done the resulting signature is published on the according MQTT topic and the next simulation run for the next node and resistance can be issued according to the schedule. The termination of a simulation is detected by subscribing to the SIGNATURES topic and comparing the generated signatures according to its node and resistance.

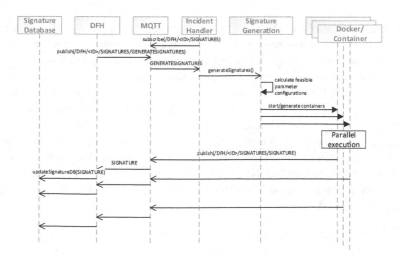

Fig. 7. Process flow of the signature generation.

The remote application running in the docker instance can be called in a parallelized manner for cases with different fault resistances and locations. The application offers a REST API implemented in Python Flask[11]. The remote application is shown in Fig. 8, it is used with an external JSON call that includes the fault resistance, fault node ID, main feeder ID and grid topology ID. Based on this information a *parameter structure.mat* is created by a function implemented in Octave[12]. The standalone application generated from the grid model in Simulink is executed with the *parameter structure.mat*. The outputs are the current and voltage signatures, which are discretized and published to a MQTT topic and then stored in the database. The REST API responds with a message of successful completion.

Signatures are created from the Simulink model of the grid that is in the standalone application by measuring the time series of voltage and current at the main feeder in a defined interval before the fault and during the transient. Then, the signatures are saved as mat files.

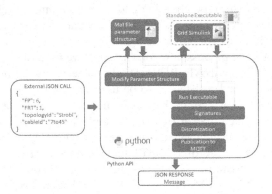

Fig. 8. Remote application.

The process flow of the Distance Determination is shown in Fig. 9. After a fault detected by the DSOs measurement device the observed measurements are stored in a database and an alarm message is published. According to the timestamp of the alarm message, additional information, like measurement series recorded around this period are requested by the EFA. In addition to the measurement series, the relevant simulated signatures are requested from the DFH or the signature database respectively. Afterwards, for the distance metric we calculate the correlations between time series data of the measurement series with every time series of the signatures using the Pearsons-correlation included in the org.apache.commons.math3 library. The results are stored in a collection of FAULTLOACTIONS DTOs. Afterwards the collection is sorted according to the correlation results and the three highest values as well as the corresponding node ID are published.

---

[11] https://flask.palletsprojects.com/en/2.0.x/.
[12] https://www.gnu.org/software/octave/index.

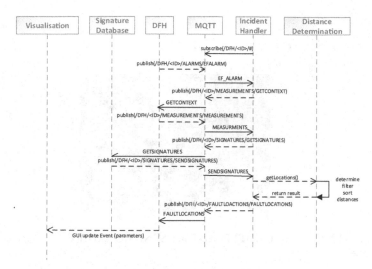

Fig. 9. Process flow of the distance determination.

4 Results and Discussion

In this section, we state evaluation results with respect to the MQTT message bus and information flow and discuss them. The evaluation shows that the proposed system provides a scalable and robust solution for fast earth fault localization. Since, the system is supposed to process hundreds of signatures during the online phase, it is required to transfer a large number of these time series data to ensure scalability and short response times. In addition, the functionality and interoperability of the DFH and the EFA should be given. Hence, the information flows of the two phases have been evaluated using different test data and messages.

4.1 MQTT Evaluation

To accelerate earth fault detection, the proposed architecture uses the MQTT protocol as a message bus. This involves sending potentially large messages over the bus. However, the MQTT protocol is originally designed for rather small messages. Consequently, we evaluate whether the messages sent in our ICT architecture fit with the message sizes supported by the MQTT protocol, which is 260MB.

The far largest messages are sent when the DFH sends signatures requested by the distance determination module. Such a message can contain around 1,000 signatures. Consequently, we create a realistic SENDSIGNATURES message, and try to publish this message on MQTT as well as check the size of this message. The SENDSIGNATURES message used for the test contains 1,000 signatures having sizes the EFA currently uses. As result, each of these signatures contains in total $200 * 6 = 1,200$ realistic measurement values between -999.99 and $+999.99$ (200 measurements for voltage and current for each phase). As result of the test, as Fig. 10 illustrates, we successfully published this message on MQTT. Moreover, the size of this message equals 11.2 MB, which is an order

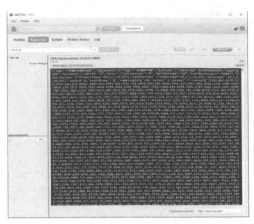

Fig. 10. External MQTT client MQTT.fx receiving SENDSIGNATURES message containing 1,000 signatures.

of magnitude smaller than the limit. This means that our architecture is robust enough to handle, e.g., up to 22,600 signatures per feeder, or 1,000 signatures containing up to 4,500 measurement values for voltage and currents per phase.

4.2 Information Flow

Both, the online and the offline phase have been implemented. The Mosquitto MQTT broker was deployed and configured. The basis of the DFH was already existing and has been extended as described in the previous sections and deployed on the same instance as the MQTT. The EFA was deployed at a remote location, from which subscribing and publishing to the MQTT broker was possible. The Standalone Application including the REST API and the compiled Simulink model was deployed on a dedicated Windows machine.

At the current state of development an external trigger, publishing an according message, was used to start the signature generation process. We could demonstrate that the expected REST API calls have been executed by the signature generation module. Afterwards the parameter structure.mat, which holds the simulation parameters, was generated and the Standalone Application was executed. The resulting signature consisting of voltage and current time series were discretized and published via MQTT. The DFH received the single signature and stored it into the signature database following the defined data model.

Also for localization, we injected an earth fault alarm message, which was published. The EFA received the message and requested measurements with a time interval according to the timestamp within the alarm message. Aside from the measurement, the signatures, previously generated and stored in the database where requested by the EFA. The signatures where selected by the DFH by the topology ID and main feeder ID. Signatures and the measurement were passed to the distance determination module, and for every signature the correlation to the measurement was calculated. The node ID and the corresponding correlation were sorted and the three locations, with the highest correlation were published. The locations were received by the visualization component of the DFH (Webapplication) and the corresponding nodes were colorized with respect to their correlation value.

The initial evaluation shows that a sufficient number of signatures can be transferred and processes by the system and the data exchange can be executed by the protocol used. Even with a bandwidth of 25MBit/s the transfer time is less than 4 s. The MQTT protocol is mature and also provides basic security features. Overall, the expected behavior of the system could demonstrated using appropriate test data and messages.

5 Conclusion and Outlook

In this paper we presented a fully operational ICT system for earth fault localization based on simulated signature values and real earth fault measurements. The required information and data is processed and the resulting fault location candidates are visualized accordingly. The proposed and implemented system is scalable, interoperable and can be easily extended. In the frame of the ongoing research project the measurement headend will be connected to a DSOs detection and monitoring equipment. By this, the observed measurements can be automatically processed and possible fault locations can be visualized. This system is designed to help the DSO to narrow down the location of the fault so that the cause can be repaired more quickly to establish the normal state of operation and prevent cascading faults. The latter ones can occur by switching operations, which are partially used to exclude the fault in certain network sections.

Future work will focus on the evaluation of the system using different topologies and to fully integrate the signature generation process, so it can be triggered based on, e.g., topology changes. Besides the approach to infer possible fault locations by calculating the correlation of simulated signatures with actual ground fault measurements, methods based on neural networks are also investigated and implemented into the distance determination module during the ongoing research project.

Acknowledgement. The software architecture and implementation presented in this paper was developed as part of the research Project EDaF (FKZ: 01IS18089) funded by the BMBF.

References

1. Wörmann, J., Tafehi, E., Duchon, M., Silva, N., Schwefel, H.-P.: Sensitivity analysis of earth fault localization. In: IEEE International Conference on Communications, Montreal (2021)
2. Chang, K.: Geographic information system. In: International Encyclopedia of Geography: People, the Earth, Environment and Technology, pp. 1–10 (2016)
3. Liu, X.L., Golab, L., Ilyas, I.: SMAS: a smart meter data analytics system. In: IEEE 31st International Conference on Data Engineering (ICDE), pp. 1476–1479. IEEE (2015)
4. Schwefel, H.-P., Silva, N.: Device and method for locating earth faults in compensated electrical. Patent EP18167395.5 (2012)
5. Nainar, K., Catalin-Iosif, C., Shahid, K., Loevenstein Olsen, R., Schäler, C., Schwefel, H.-P.: Experimental validation and deployment of observability applications for monitoring of low-voltage distribution grids. In: Sensors, MDPI (2021, to appear)

6. Tex, C., Hertweck, P., Schäler, M., Böhm, K.: PrivEnergy: a privacy operator framework addressing individual concerns. In: Proceedings of the Ninth International Conference on Future Energy Systems (e-Energy), pp. 426–428. IEEE (2018)
7. Tex, C., Schäler, M., Böhm, K.: Swellfish privacy: exploiting time-dependent relevance for continuous differential privacy. KIT Scientific Working Papers, Karlsruhe (2020)
8. Brockmann, C., et al.: Monitoringsystem für Verteilnetztrassen zur Ortsbestimmung von Erdfehlern an Hochspannungsfreileitungen (2017)
9. Steurer, H., Fickert, L., Schmautzer, E.: Einführung eines neuen Erdschlussortungs-Systems KNOPE und erste Erfahrungen. In: e & i Elektrotechnik und Informationstechnik (2014)
10. Schmauss, B., Werzinger, S.: Verbundprojekt: iMonet - Intelligentes Monitoring von Betriebsanlagen für künftige Stromnetze: Teilvorhaben iMonet: Erarbeitung wissenschaftlicher Grundlagen, Lehrstuhl für Hochfrequenztechnik (LHFT) der Friedrich-Alexander-Universität Erlangen-Nürnberg (2017)
11. Safargholi, F., et al.: Optimierte Effizienz und Netzverträglichkeit bei der Integration von Erzeugungsanlagen aus Oberschwingungssicht : Abschlussbericht für das Projekt NetzHarmonie (2019)
12. Light, R.A.: Mosquitto: server and client implementation of the MQTT protocol. J. Open Source Softw. **13**, 265 (2017)
13. Ilias Gerostathopoulos, C.P.T.B.: Adapting a system with noisy outputs with statistical guarantee. In: International Symposium on Software Engineering for Adaptive and Self-Managing Systems (SEAMS 2018) (2018)
14. Schmid, S., Gerostathopoulos, I., Prehofer, C., Bures, T.: Self-adaptation based on big data analytics: a model problem and tool. In: International Symposium on Software Engineering for Adaptive and Self-Managing Systems (SEAMS 2017) (2017)
15. Horn, D., Bischl, B.: Multi-objective parameter configuration of machine learning algorithms using model-based. In: Symposium Series on Computational Intelligence (SSCI), pp. 1–8. IEEE (2016)

Power Loss Reduction in Low-Voltage Distribution Grids via Coordinated Reactive Power Management of PV Inverters

Yonghao Gui[1]([✉]), Hans-Peter Schwefel[2,3], Jan Dimon Bendtsen[1],
and Jakob Stoustrup[1]

[1] Automation and Control Section at the Department of Electronic Systems,
Aalborg University, 9220 Aalborg, Denmark
{yg,dimon,jakob}@es.aau.dk
[2] Wireless Communication Networks Section at the Department of Electronic
Systems, Aalborg University, 9220 Aalborg, Denmark
hps@es.aau.dk
[3] GridData GmbH, Anger/Traunstein, Germany

Abstract. Reducing technical energy losses in the distribution grid has
a direct economic benefit for the distribution system operator and furthermore it can increase the grid hosting capacity. Part of the technical
losses is due to reactive power in the distribution grid. The approach
in this paper is to centrally calculate optimized configurations for local
$Q(V)$ control of grid-connected inverters, with the target to reduced technical losses in the low voltage grid. The preliminary assessment in this
short paper shows that there is a potential of up to 19.8% loss reduction
for a realistic low voltage feeder.

Keywords: Coordinated control · Distribution grids · Power loss ·
Photovoltaics

1 Introduction

Due to high resistance-to-reactance ratio and high currents in low voltage distribution grids, the power losses tend to be relatively high compared with the
transmission system [11]. Hence, reduction of power losses in the distribution
grid is one of the significant issues. Various methods have been proposed to
reduce the power losses, e.g., grid topology adjustments [1], capacitor banks [5],
and distributed generators [10].

Recently, more and more renewable energy sources (e.g., PV and wind) are
integrated into the distribution grids, in particular PV-based distributed generators are installed rapidly to meet the green energy demands in the European

The research leading to these results has received funding from the European Union's
Horizon 2020 research and innovation programme under grant agreement No. 774145
for the Net2DG Project (www.net2dg.eu).

R. Adler et al. (Eds.): EDCC 2021 Workshops, CCIS 1462, pp. 65–72, 2021.
https://doi.org/10.1007/978-3-030-86507-8_6

Union [12]. The evolution of technology of power converters [6–8] provides opportunities to utilize the inverter capabilities to reduce power losses and reduced grid congestion.

In addition, the introduction of communication interfaces to the inverters allows for centralized coordination of inverter settings, such that power losses can be minimized by managing the reactive power of PV systems efficiently, for instance by having the PV systems near the substation produce reactive power to reduce the power flow as well as the power losses in the grid [14, 15]. When using Volt-VAR local control, PV inverters near the substation, on the other hand, may be forced to work under unit power factor, since it has a lower sensitivity value than those at the end of the feeder [4]. This means that the reactive power of the PV inverter may be wasted, which could otherwise have been used for, e.g., reducing power losses.

In this paper, a Control Coordination (CC) application of local $Q(V)$ control of PV inverters is proposed with the target to reduced technical losses in the low voltage grid. An objective function focusing on minimization of power losses is designed to generate optimal set-points to those PV inverters. The proposed method is validated in a representative Danish low voltage feeder. The result shows that the proposed CC application has a potential ability to reduce 19.8% power losses.

2   Control Coordination Application and Local Control

The CC application can be designed to maintain voltages within the predefined bound in distribution grid through updating set-points of $Q(V)$ local control of each PV inverter[8]. For the purpose of this paper, a different objective function with the aim of to minimizing the power loss in the distribution grid is introduced and added into the CC application, which calculates the optimal set-points of $Q(V)$ local control of each PV inverter.

2.1 $Q(V)$ Local Control at Inverters

In this paper, $Q(V)$ control shown in Fig. 1(a) is used in each PV inverter as a local controller, which can be formulated such as

$$Q_{PV} = \begin{cases} Q_{\max}, & V_{PV} < V_a \\ \kappa\,(V_{PV} - V_a)\,, & V_a \leq V_{PV} \leq V_b \\ 0, & V_b \leq V_{PV} \leq V_c \\ \kappa\,(V_{PV} - V_c)\,, & V_c \leq V_{PV} \leq V_d \\ Q_{\min}, & V_{PV} > V_d \end{cases} \tag{1}$$

where $\kappa = \frac{Q_{\max}}{V_a - V_b}\,(V_{PV} - V_a)$ represents the droop coefficient. The CC application calculates the optimal set-points of $Q(V)$ to minimize the power losses, and sends them to each PV inverter. Then, $Q(V)$ control in (1) is changed as shown

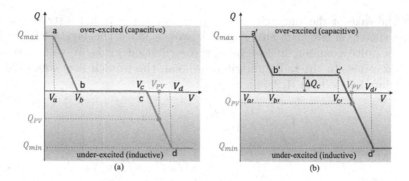

Fig. 1. (a) Default $Q(V)$ control in the PV inverter; (b) $Q(V)$ control corrected by CC application.

in Fig. 1(b). Normally, the voltage at the end of the feeder has an over-voltage issue when the PV system has a peak power, and the voltage near the substation is close the voltage at the substation. Consequently, the PV inverter at the end of the feeder has to operate in the inductive mode to avoid the over-voltage issue, and the PV inverter near the substation can operate in the capacitive mode to minimize the power losses through minimizing reactive power flow in the distribution grid, as shown in Fig. 2.

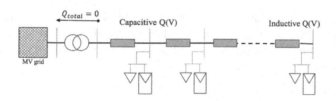

Fig. 2. Loss minimization and voltage reduction in the distribution grid.

2.2   Loss Minimization

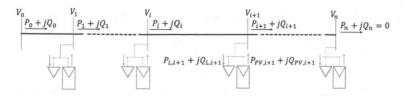

Fig. 3. Power flow in a radial low voltage distribution grid with loads and PVs.

For the sake of the simplicity, we only consider the radial distribution grid segment shown in Fig. 3 in this paper; however, since the layout of this grid section is quite common in low voltage distribution grids, it will serve as a generic example. In the radial distribution grid, the branch flow equations can be formulated as follows [1,2,14]:

$$P_{i+1} = P_i - r_i \frac{P_i^2 + Q_i^2}{V_i^2} - P_{L,i+1} + P_{PV,i+1} \tag{2}$$

$$Q_{i+1} = Q_i - x_i \frac{P_i^2 + Q_i^2}{V_i^2} - Q_{L,i+1} + Q_{PV,i+1} \tag{3}$$

$$V_{i+1}^2 = V_i^2 - 2\left(r_i P_i + x_i Q_i\right) + \left(r_i^2 + x_i^2\right) \frac{P_i^2 + Q_i^2}{V_i^2} \tag{4}$$

where P_i and Q_i are the active and reactive power flows and r_i and x_i are the line resistance and reactance from node i to $i+1$, respectively. V_i is the voltage magnitude at node i. Furthermore, $P_{L,i+1}$ and $Q_{L,i+1}$ are the active and reactive power of the load at node $i+1$, and $P_{PV,i+1}$ and $Q_{PV,i+1}$ are the active and reactive power of the PV system at node $i+1$, respectively.

The active power losses in the distribution grid is defined as follow [2]:

$$\mathcal{L}(\mathbf{x}, \mathbf{u}) = \sum_{i=0}^{n-1} r_i \frac{P_i^2 + Q_i^2}{V_i^2}. \tag{5}$$

Minimizing power losses in (5) as much as possible is one of the main targets in the distribution grid. In order to reduce the computational burden of the above optimization, we need a simple version of power flows in (2) to (4) as follows [15]:

$$P_{i+1} = P_i - P_{L,i+1} + P_{PV,i+1} \tag{6}$$

$$Q_{i+1} = Q_i - Q_{L,i+1} + Q_{PV,i+1} \tag{7}$$

$$V_{i+1} = V_i - \frac{(r_i P_i + x_i Q_i)}{V_0} \tag{8}$$

Consequently, the power losses can be simplified as

$$\mathcal{L}(\mathbf{x}, \mathbf{u}) = \sum_{i=0}^{n-1} r_i \frac{P_i^2 + Q_i^2}{V_0^2} \tag{9}$$

The objective of minimization of power losses can be formulated such as

$$\min_{P,Q,P_{PV},Q_{PV},V} \mathcal{L}(\mathbf{x}, \mathbf{u}) \tag{10}$$

$$\text{s.t. eqs. (6)-(8).}$$

In addition, the reactive power capacity of PV inverter should be considered.

$$Q_{PV}^{\min} \leq Q_{PV,i} \leq Q_{PV}^{\max}, \ \forall i. \tag{11}$$

Here, we consider that $Q_{PV}^{\min \& \max}$ is ± 0.53 pu [8]. From (9), it can be observed that the minimization of power losses is to decrease the reactive power flow since one of the most important targets is extract the active power from PV systems as much as possible. Consequently, the minimization of power losses changes to the following simple form.

$$\min_{P,Q,P_{PV},Q_{PV}} \sum_{i=0}^{n-1} r_i \frac{Q_i^2}{V_0^2} \tag{12}$$

$$\text{s.t. eqs. (6)-(8).}$$

Thanks to the smart meters deployed in the distribution grid, the CC application can calculate the optimized setpoints and communicate them to the PV inverters see Fig. 4.

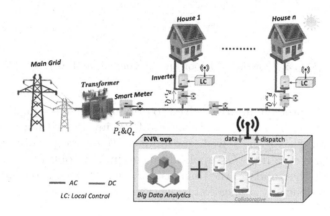

Fig. 4. Control Coordination application implementation in the low voltage distribution grid via communication.

Another target is to maintain the voltage within the limits defined by the grid code [13]. It can be observed from (8) that the voltage magnitude varies based on the active and reactive power flows. E.g., if there exists a reverse active power flow (i.e., $P_{L,i} < P_{PV,i}$), the voltage at the node i is increased. In this case, we can use the reactive power generated by the PV inverter to compensate for that voltage violation. The objective function of voltage violation can be found in [8].

2.3   Flowchart of Control Coordination Application

An overview of the CC application is presented in Fig. 5. At each sample time instant k, the CC application receives all the data including voltage, active power, and reactive power of smart meters and PV inverters via communication. Then, check whether or not the voltage is within the certain bound. If yes,

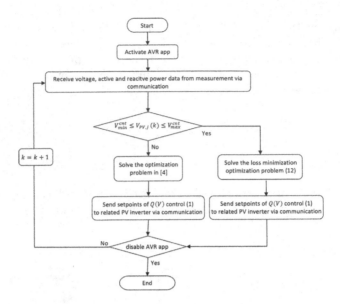

Fig. 5. Flowchart of coordinated control application.

the optimization problem in (9) is solved to obtain optimal set-points of the PV inverters. Then, update $Q(V)$ local control of PV inverter. If no, the optimization problem in [8] is to be solved, and updates the corresponding $Q(V)$ local control of PV inverter. If the CC application continues to optimize the operation of PV inverters, then updates the time instant, i.e., $k+1$ and continues the first step. Otherwise, the CC application is deactivated.

3   Case Study

In this Section, for the purpose of loss minimization, Feeder 5 of the Danish field trial grid from Net2DG, shown in Fig. 6, is used to test the effectiveness of the CC application. It should be noted that the capacity of the PV inverters is modified compared with the original one. The capacity of each PV inverter is assumed as 5 kVA. The default setting of $Q(V)$ control is $V_a = 0.9$ pu, $V_b = 0.95$ pu, $V_c = 1.05$ pu, $V_d = 1.1$ pu and $Q_a = 0.53$ pu, $Q_{b,c} = 0$ pu, $Q_d = -0.53$ pu [3].

3.1   Loss Minimization

For the sake of the simplicity, a high load operation condition is tested the availability and effectiveness of loss minimization of the CC application, i.e., the power values at the substation are $P = 35.45$ kW & $Q = 25.74$ kVar [9]. Figure 7 shows that the total power loss within Feeder 5 without the CC application is 0.95 kW. However, when the CC application is activated at 40 s, the total power loss in the grid is decreased to 0.76 kW, which is a 19.8% reduction.

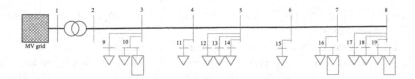

Fig. 6. Feeder 5 of the field trial grid in Denmark [8].

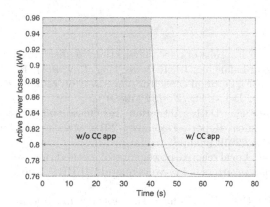

Fig. 7. Loss minimization with and without the CC application.

3.2   Discussion

From the above result, it can be seen that the CC application has the ability to significantly reduce the power loss in the distribution grid. The amount of the loss minimization depends on the capacity of the PV inverters and on the reactive power flows in the distribution grid. For example, when the PV inverters use their maximum reactive power capability to reduce reactive power flow, the power loss is minimized the most by the PV inverters. In addition, managing the active power of PV inverters can reduce the power loss in the grid as well despite reduction of PV owners benefits. However, it can be handled by using energy storage systems to manage the active power efficiently, which leads to keeping local balance, i.e., reducing the active power flow in the grid.

4   Conclusions and Future Works

In this paper, a modified CC application for PV inverters has been presented to not only reduce power losses but also keep the voltages within the certain limit in the low voltage distribution grid. The CC application is designed to manage the reactive power flows efficiently in the low voltage distribution grid in order to reduce the power losses. In the CC application, the optimal set-points of the Volt-VAR local control are calculated centrally for the LV grid area and sent to each PV inverter. The propose method was validated in a Danish representative low voltage distribution grid, in which the proposed CC application can decrease the power losses 19.8%.

In the future works, realistic consumption and generation profiles over longer periods will be used to verify the effectiveness of reduction of power losses via the CC application and additional representative grids with more PV systems will be used to test the proposed method.

References

1. Baran, M., Wu, F.F.: Network reconfiguration in distribution systems for loss reduction and load balancing. IEEE Power Eng. Rev. **9**(4), 101–102 (1989)
2. Baran, M., Wu, F.F.: Optimal capacitor placement on radial distribution systems. IEEE Trans. Power Del. **4**(1), 725–734 (1989)
3. Bendtsen, J., et al.: D4.1: Actuation Schemes and Control Coordination Approaches. Technical Report, December 2019. www.net2dg.eu/wafx_res/Files/Net2DG_D4.1_27.12.2019_final.pdf
4. Demirok, E., et al.: Local reactive power control methods for overvoltage prevention of distributed solar inverters in low-voltage grids. IEEE J. Photovolt. **1**(2), 174–182 (2011)
5. Devabalaji, K.R., Ravi, K., Kothari, D.: Optimal location and sizing of capacitor placement in radial distribution system using bacterial foraging optimization algorithm. Int. J. Electr. Power Energy Syst. **71**, 383–390 (2015)
6. Gui, Y., Blaabjerg, F., Wang, X., Bendtsen, J., Yang, D., Stoustrup, J.: Improved DC-link voltage regulation strategy for grid-connected converters. IEEE Trans. Ind. Electron. **68**(6), 4977–4987 (2021)
7. Gui, Y., Wang, X., Blaabjerg, F., Pan, D.: Control of grid-connected voltage-source-converters: relationship between direct-power-control and vector-current-control. IEEE Trans. Ind. Electron. Mag. **13**(2), 31–40 (2019)
8. Gui, Y., Bendtsen, J.D., Stoustrup, J.: Coordinated control of pv inverters in distribution grid using local and centralized control. In: 46th Annual Conference IEEE Industrial Electronic Society (IECON), pp. 1773–1778 (2020)
9. Nainar, K., et al.: Deployment of observability applications in low-voltage distribution grids-A practical approach. Sensors (2021 submitted)
10. Rao, R.S., Ravindra, K., Satish, K., Narasimham, S.: Power loss minimization in distribution system using network reconfiguration in the presence of distributed generation. IEEE Trans. Power Syst. **28**(1), 317–325 (2013)
11. Sambaiah, K.S., Jayabarathi, T.: Loss minimization techniques for optimal operation and planning of distribution systems: a review of different methodologies. Int. Trans. Electr. Energy Syst. **30**(2), e12230 (2020)
12. SolarPower Europe: Global Market Outlook For Solar Power 2020–2024. Technical Report, December 2020. https://www.solarpowereurope.org/european-market-outlook-for-solar-power-2020-2024/
13. Sun, H., et al.: Review of challenges and research opportunities for voltage control in smart grids. IEEE Trans. Power Syst. **34**(4), 2790–2801 (2019)
14. Turitsyn, K., Šulc, P., Backhaus, S., Chertkov, M.: Distributed control of reactive power flow in a radial distribution circuit with high photovoltaic penetration. In: IEEE PES General Meeting, pp. 1–6. IEEE (2010)
15. Yeh, H., Gayme, D.F., Low, S.H.: Adaptive VAR control for distribution circuits with photovoltaic generators. IEEE Trans. Power Syst. **27**(3), 1656–1663 (2012)

Enabling a Zero Trust Architecture in Smart Grids Through a Digital Twin

Giovanni Paolo Sellitto[1]([✉]), Helder Aranha[2], Massimiliano Masi[3], and Tanja Pavleska[4]

[1] Rome, Italy
[2] Lisbon, Portugal
[3] Tiani "Spirit" GmbH, Vienna, Austria
massimiliano.masi@tiani-spirit.com
[4] Jozef Stefan Institute, Ljubljana, Slovenia
atanja@e5.ijs.si

Abstract. In this work, we draft a methodology to build a cyber-security digital twin of a Smart Grid, starting from its architectural blueprint. The idea of a digital twin is not new and has recently been proposed as a means to enable simulations for the purpose of environmental protection where tests on the real system are difficult or expensive. The novelty in our work is in proposing and analyzing the possibility to dynamically align the digital twin with its real counterpart. As a preliminary step toward the synthesis of a Digital Twin for the Smart Grid, we propose the adoption of an architectural view that gets dynamically aligned with the state of the world at deploy and operation time. In this manner, we lay out the basis for a maintenance-aware model, which is at the core of the "digital twin" concept. The availability of a digital twin allows the enforcement of policies for the devices when they connect to the Grid. This paves the way for a *Zero Trust Architecture* (ZTA), as introduced in this work.

Keywords: Smart Grids · Security-by-design · Zero Trust Architecture · Digital Twin

1 Introduction

In a previous work [1], we presented a methodology to enable security by design in Smart Grids. It combined a modular Smart Grid Architectural Model (SGAM) with a cybersecurity evaluation cycle based on the Reference Model for Information Assurance and Security (RMIAS). Its aim was to facilitate the automatic evaluation of the quality attributes and security properties of the Smart Grid architecture. There, the security development cycle leveraged a process of continuous validation, allowing for a formal description and automated evaluation

G. P. Sellitto and H. Aranha—Independent Scholars.

R. Adler et al. (Eds.): EDCC 2021 Workshops, CCIS 1462, pp. 73–81, 2021.
https://doi.org/10.1007/978-3-030-86507-8_7

of the resulting architecture. However, the Smart Grid has become heavily based on off-the-shelves products that are connected to the infrastructure on the fly. As a result, the design phases are loosing their importance due to the modular architecture that remains stable for a long time and offers standard interfaces to favour the connection of new users to the Grid. In addition, as the number of Distributed Energy Resources (DER) and prosumers that are connecting to the grid increases, the Grid's architecture model is changing from a "hub and spoke" with a limited number of central Distribution System Operator (DSO)[1] to a more dynamic model. This dynamic allows the actors to choose at each moment if they will play the role of a consumer or of a producer and which virtual distribution network they will join.

In such environment, the adoption of development operations and artefacts that can be used for the governance of the Smart Grid along the entire lifecycle is of paramount importance. As we realized during the recent COVID-19 global pandemic, which has forced businesses to adopt remote workforces and establish new operations protocols, the demand for traditional and labor intensive operations has been reduced and will be rapidly replaced by smart utility applications. Remote monitoring of the Distributed Energy Resources (DERs) and a major focus on reducing consumption are becoming the new trends for Smart Grids. However, they demand new architectural solutions, especially in the domain of data and service exchange. This has a direct impact on the design of the Smart Grid security. In this paper, we make a leap forward from the existing work, developing a "cybersecurity digital twin" for the Smart Grid. To this purpose, we will draft a methodology to derive the Digital Twin from the architectural blueprint of the smart grid and to augment it with information regarding the effective topology of the assets at deploy time, maintaining it aligned with the real twin over the operation lifecycle. The transformation will leverage the definition of a specific viewpoint, called the Control Viewpoint that will group together all the components needed to build the Digital Twin and to keep it aligned with the Smart Grid. The rest of this paper is organized as follows: Sect. 2 briefly sketches the current state of the methodology developed in our previous work, merging standardized models in view of the architectural requirements and the modelling specifications relevant for Smart Grids. Section 3 presents the methodology upgrades by introducing the concept of control view, digital twin and zero-trust architecture in the context of Smart Grids. An overview of Related work is given in Sect. 4 to position our proposal among the state of the art approaches. Finally, Sect. 5 touches upon future work and concludes the paper.

---

[1] Distribution System Operators (DSOs) are the operating managers (and sometimes owners) of energy distribution networks, operating at low, medium or high voltage levels.

2 Current State of the Methodology

In this section, we re-capture the basics of the methodology provided by our work so far, and then explain how this paper upgrades the current state to meet the goals outlined in the introduction.

In [1], we presented a multidimensional framework for Information Assurance and Security to enable cybersecurity by design in the Smart Grid (SG). The Smart Grid Architectural Model (SGAM) [2] provides a modular reference architecture where components could, in principle, be easily combined, checked and turned into software products, reducing time-to-market and lowering the adoption barriers for prospective DER owners. However, building solution architectures based on SGAM is currently a fully manual task: the architect must select the suited solutions and consider all the inter-dependencies among the components and the variability points in order to design a cohesive and inter-operable solution. In addition, while SGAM accounts for cybersecurity and privacy in Smart Grids in a standardized manner (see the CG-SEG report in [3]), it lacks a generic (context independent) methodology to facilitate the enforcement of adequate security levels. To address these issues, we introduced *MOdular Security-Aware ADL*, MOSA². It is an architecture description language (ADL) to be used at design time to: (a) describe architecture building blocks in terms of profiles, (b) specify interactions among them, and (c) semi-automatically create input to verify the fulfillment of quality constraints with formal methods.

The security development cycle required the initial definition of an architecture and the specification of quality attributes by using MOSA² constructs [4]. Additional modular security (sub)constructs were also integrated into the architecture, following the RMIAS process [5]:

- Per profile, identifying information assets to protect with the help of well-defined taxonomies;
- Mapping the former into information categories;
- Performing risk analysis to prioritize the security goals appropriate for each category according to the business needs; and
- Identifying and selecting cost-effective security countermeasures to fulfill the security goals for each category.

As part of this framework, a fully automated process guided by a formal semantic model builds the code to be used for further analysis, but also to specify the evaluation protocol. The latter is done using SMT-LIB [6]². Then, the Z3 solver³ was employed to provide a formal proof for supporting the architectural security goals. By iterating through this process, a system designer can *refactor* the architecture while having a formal proof on whether the security goals and the quality service level agreements are met by design or not.

The RMIAS-based process was used to find the best countermeasures an organization can afford to protect important information assets from identified

---

² We use the SMT-LIB specifications since they are standard and adopted by most of the SMT solvers available.

³ See https://github.com/Z3Prover/z3.

categories of cyberthreats. While the proposed language MOSA[2] leverages the modular architectural constructs to allow for automated security evaluation,[4] the process was equally applicable to SGAM-based architectural processes that do not necessarily embrace modularity to design Smart Grid functionalities. This approach is well suited for architects but it suffers some limitations. Although it was tailored to address security by design, it offers very little flexibility when the grid has been deployed. This happens since *security by design* hardly allows for any deviation from specifications and blueprints during operations.

3   Proposed Upgrade of the Methodology

To overcome the limitations described above, in this section we extend the current methodology with a *Control View* and a *Digital Twin*. Then we also explain how Zero-trust architecture is also supported by this upgrade. The Control View is an architectural construct defined at the Functional layer of the SGAM model and materialized as an architecture view. Its role is mainly to observe and react upon the addition or removal of DERs to and from the grid, and, ultimately, maintaining a **desired level of trust** among the DERs and the Grid at large. In Sect. 3.1 we explain how to generate the artefacts materializing this function. The *Digital Twin*[5] is an artefact generated according to an *architecture viewpoint* that addresses the concern for cybersecurity, enabling threat modeling over the full Smart Grid lifecycle: design, provisioning and operation.

3.1   The Control View

The Control View (CV)[6] offers the means to virtualize DERs in an automated manner using the proxy pattern, and register/unregister them at runtime. When a new DER is added to the Smart Grid, a proxy of the DER is deployed using a *sidecar* pattern [7]. The sidecar pattern splits the application logic of a DER over two containers: the application container and a sidecar container, which adds functionality that otherwise might be difficult to include in the application container. The adoption of this pattern is aimed to decouple the Smart Grid application or business logic from grid overlay functions, focusing on the business level architectural features. Thus, the work of the architecture team is decoupled from the tasks in charge of the DER operators, the prosumers and the operation team. Thus, the architecture and design team can focus on the development and test of Solution Architectural Templates, while the management team will benefit from a tool that can support operations under the disciplined approach of the SG Enterprise Architecture.

---

[4] The language is implemented and available at http://github.com/mascanc.

[5] The Digital Twin could be seen as a view in itself, but in this case it gains the status of an autonomous concept, a sort of personified notion.

[6] To highlight the underlying concern, we choose to define a specific view, instead of recurring to existing architectural views, but this artefact can be implemented as a function.

The artefacts associated with the CV can be derived in a semi-automatic manner from the Architectural Blueprint of the Smart Grid (EA) and a pseudo algorithm is sketched in Algorithm 1. The employment of sidecar container also allows to depart from the traditional Smart Grid Security approach, which is based on a strong perimeter to prevent unauthorized access. Nevertheless, this view is still supported by the architectural artefacts obtained from the application of the same modelling patterns as for the other SGAM layers: Information, Communication, etc.

Although the design benefits brought about by the CV are great, it has mainly been introduced to build the digital twin of the Smart Grid and to (actively and dynamically) feed relevant data into the digital twin.

Algorithm 1: From EA to Control View

Data: An Architectural Model (EA) $\mathcal{A}$ of the Smart Grid
Result: A Control View $\mathcal{C}$, containing a proxy for each DER and device in the Smart Grid
1 Let $\mathcal{C} = \emptyset$ be the initial Control View;
2 Let $\mathcal{P} = \emptyset$ be set of active DER *proxies* at runtime;
3 **DESIGN PHASE:**
4 /*At design time, provide the templates to instantiate the *proxy* elements for each DER, to build the Control View, */
5 **foreach** *DER der* $\in \mathcal{A}$ **do**
6 | provide a *proxy* using the sidecar pattern;
7 | define security policies
8 **end**
9 **PROVISIONING PHASE:**
10 **foreach** *DER der* $\in$ Smart Grid **do**
11 | enforce policies
12 | add the specific *proxy* to $\mathcal{C}$
13 | return $\mathcal{C}$
14 **end**
15 **OPERATION PHASE:**
16 **repeat**
17 | whenever a DER joins the Smart Grid: check policies, activate its *proxy*
18 | whenever a DER leaves: deactivate its proxy
19 | update $\mathcal{P}$
20 **until** *forever*;

3.2   The Digital Twin

The concept of a digital twin denotes a *"model that mirrors a unique physical object, process, organization, person or other abstraction. Data from multiple digital twins can be aggregated for a composite view across a number of real-world entities, such as a power plant or a city, and their related processes"* [8].

It is a "representation in a virtual space of a physical structure in real space and the information flow between the two that keeps them synchronized". The introduction of the CV enables the management of information flow needed for the dynamic alignment of the digital twin with the real Smart Grid. This is possible since every new participant that joins the grid is registered through the sidecar and its state is monitored until it gets de-registered.

The CV also offers the tools to analyze and control the behavior of the grid at runtime and to transfer the relevant data to the digital twin, enabling the possibility to gather data and analyze the behavior of the system to control it. The possibility to continuously synchronize the digital model with the Grid through an information flow mediated by the CV is the main upgrade that we propose in this paper. This feature paves the way for a Maintenance Aware approach to Development. A pseudo-algorithm that can be used to derive a digital twin from the control view is sketched in Algorithm 2.

Algorithm 2: Build and Manage the Digital Twin from Control View

---

    Data: A Control View $\mathcal{C}$, containing a proxy for each DER and device in the Smart Grid

    Result: A Digital Twin, modeling the Smart grid, $\mathcal{T} \cup \mathcal{F}$, the Information Flows needed to keep it dynamically aligned with the Smart Grid

1   Let $\mathcal{T} = \emptyset$ the initial Digital Twin;

2   Let $\mathcal{F} = \emptyset$ the initial set of Flows;

3   **DESIGN PHASE:**

4   /*In addition to the *proxy* elements to build the Control View, provide the architectural templates *twin* and *flow* to build the Digital Twin */

5   **foreach** *DER der* $\in \mathcal{D}$ **do**

6   provide a *twin* (digital model)

7   define the *flow* templates to keep the twin up-to-date;

8   **end**

9   **PROVISIONING PHASE:**

10   **foreach** *proxy* $\in \mathcal{C}$ **do**

11   add the specific *twin* to $\mathcal{T}$

12   add the relevant *flows* to $\mathcal{F}$;

13   return $\mathcal{T} \cup \mathcal{F}$

14   **end**

15   **OPERATION PHASE:**

16   **foreach** *relevant event triggered according to policies* **do**

17   **repeat**

18   **foreach** *flow* $\in \mathcal{F}$ **do**

19   let *twin'* = update (*twin*)

20   return ($\mathcal{T}$ - twin) U *twin'*

21   **end**

22   **until** *all twin* $\in \mathcal{T}$ *are up to date*;

23   **end**

3.3 Leveraging DT and CV for a Zero Trust Architecture

As sketched above, we can produce a Digital Twin of the Smart Grid from the CV and maintain it dynamically aligned with the real twin. The applications of the digital twin are not limited only to those documented here. A number of functionalities can also be extracted to factor out other concerns in running DERs, such as: monitoring, networking, and security. They can also be made transparent for the prosumers connected to the grid.

However, the main improvement offered by the adoption of a CV and the digital twin over the previous methodology is the possibility to support a *zero trust* Architecture (ZTA) [9]. In a ZTA, it is no longer assumed that anything within a specific security perimeter is trusted. Instead, we assume that the network is compromised and we are unaware of who, where and how it happened. Thus, everything is to be verified. In this case, the only trusted perimeter is within each DER, while anything else is non-trusted, even if it is within the same network.

Establishing trust requires the management of certificates for services and workloads, as well as service authentication and authorization. The Control View and the Digital Twin enable the DSO and the DER operators to enforce policies, like mutual TLS, to ensure encrypted traffic between each other and to help prevent person-in-the-middle attacks. With the implementation of the CV and the sidecar container, it becomes less complex to adopt a ZTA approach, since the registration in the control view helps the DSO to provide authentication and authorization identities to each DER through a central certificate authority. The certificate authorities and the availability of certificates let developers implement authorization policies that provide fine-grained control over which DERs and services can communicate.

4 Related Work

Over the last year, the architectural model of **Service Mesh** [10] is gaining ground in microservices architectures. A service mesh is a configurable Architectural Building Block that handles communication among services. A service mesh is usually implemented using a sidecar pattern, where a proxy instance is defined for each service instance. Sidecars handle interservice communications, monitoring and security–related concerns. The architectural patterns underlying a Service Mesh were adopted in our work. A well known market level examples of open source service mesh is Istio. In the context of architectural models, some approaches similar to ours have also been proposed [11,12] However, they follow the typical modular approach of the enterprise architecture [13], defining functionalities and architectural assets "wrapped" by specific containers named *building blocks* (in our approach interchanged with the concept of profiles) and a composition method to build a *solution* architecture. Our approach does not only belong to the Energy domain - it can be shared among different verticals [14].

The dynamical nature of the proposed digital twin is the main difference from the recent Visual Security development environments, which are used for risk-based protection of Critical infrastructures. In fact, they do not consider in-depth the highly dynamical nature of the grid. As a results, they not only disregard that an attacker could compromise more than one node at the same time, but also that an attack could leverage other structural weaknesses of the grid. This proposal empowers the architect with a toolchain that enables continuous validation of the resulting architecture and an ex-ante evaluation of any additional components. Automating the tool chain by exploiting a fully implemented formal language encourages such test-driven architectural design approach.

Mandated by the European Commission, the joint group CEN-CENELEC-ETSI introduced SGAM to provide a holistic architectural view on Smart Grids. SGAM is meant as an enabler for establishing Smart Grids in Europe, which the member states and the individual projects are encouraged to follow [15]. Adopting such an architectural model is crucial not only to fulfill the Availability of a resource (DER in our case), but also to avoid the effect of *vendor lock-in*.

5   Conclusion and Future Work

In this paper, an architecture-based methodology to build a cybersecurity digital twin for Smart Grids was presented. The novelty in our work is in proposing to dynamically tune the digital twin fidelity and align it with its real counterpart at both deploy and operation time. The basis for a maintenance-aware model is thus established, which is at the core of the upgraded methodology. The methodology also provides constructs for the dynamic enforcement of security policies to reflect the Smart Grid topology changes over time. These policy checking constructs enable the adoption of *Zero Trust Architecture* (ZTA).

The availability of a digital twin is also desirable since it paves the ground for probabilistic verification methods based on Agent Based Modeling (ABM) simulations. Simulations can be performed both during the design and during the operation phase and they scale better than model checking, since they run for a predefined and constant number of cycles, to be repeated under different initial or environmental conditions. In this manner, differently from what happens with model checking, the computational complexity of running simulations does not depend heavily on the size of the system under test. In the design phase, simulations support a risk-based development strategy and are focused on the architectural templates. When dealing with a pervasive system, the simulations are used to forecast and prevent attacks and to improve the dependability of the network as a whole, even with the use of visual security tools. As our methodology is goal-based rather than a threat-based, there is a need for inductive reasoning when dealing with relatively innovative systems like the Smart Grid, where we do not have a long record of incidents. Therefore, as part of our future work we will investigate the possibility to further enrich the methodology with forecasting security vulnerabilities and properties based on past system behavior.

References

1. Pavleska, T., Aranha, H., Masi, M., Sellitto, G.P.: Drafting a cybersecurity framework profile for smart grids in EU: a goal-based methodology. In: Bernardi, S., et al. (eds.) EDCC 2020. CCIS, vol. 1279, pp. 143–155. Springer, Cham (2020). https://doi.org/10.1007/978-3-030-58462-7_12
2. Smart Grid Coordination Group: Smart grid reference architecture. Technical report, vol. 2012. CEN-CENELEC-ETSI, November 2012
3. SG-CG/M490/: Smart Grid Information Security. Standard, CEN, CENELEC, ETSI, December 2014
4. Masi, M., Pavleska, T., Aranha, H.: Automating smart grid solution architecture design. In: 2018 IEEE International Conference on Communications, Control, and Computing Technologies for Smart Grids, SmartGridComm 2018, Aalborg, Denmark, 29–31 October 2018, pp. 1–6. IEEE (2018)
5. Cherdantseva, Y., Hilton, J.: A reference model of information assurance & security. In: Proceedings of the 2013 International Conference on Availability, Reliability and Security, ARES 2013, pp. 546–555. IEEE Computer Society, USA (2013)
6. Barrett, C., Stump, A., Tinelli, C.: The SMT-LIB standard: Version 2.0. Technical report, University of Iowa (2010)
7. Burns, B.: Designing Distributed Systems: Patterns and Paradigms for Scalable, Reliable Services. O'Reilly Media Inc., Sebastopol (2018)
8. Gartner Corp.: GridWise Interoperability Context-Setting Framework. Standard, GridWise Architecture Council, March 2021
9. Zero Trust Architecture. White paper, NIST, August 2020
10. Wolff, E., Prinz, H.: Service Mesh Primer. Leanpub, Victoria, BC, Canada (2019)
11. NIST: Framework and Roadmap of Smart Grid Interoperability Standards, Release 4.0 (2020)
12. OpenADR Alliance: OpenADR 2.0a Profile Specification (2020)
13. The Open Group: TOGAF 9.2 (2019)
14. European Commission ISA2: European Interoperability Reference Architecture (2020)
15. Gottschalk, M., Uslar, M., Delfs, C.: The Use Case and Smart Grid Architecture Model Approach: The IEC 62559-2 Use Case Template and the SGAM Applied in Various Domains, 1st edn. Springer, Heidelberg (2017)

Field Test Validation of Low Voltage Grid Applications in a Danish Setting

Kamal Shahid[1(✉)], Rasmus Løvenstein Olsen[1], and Rolf Kirk[2]

[1] Aalborg University, Aalborg, Denmark
ksh@es.aau.dk, rlo@es.aau.com
[2] Thy-Mors Energi, Thisted, Denmark
rok@thymors.dk

Abstract. Among various solutions, smart IT based solutions are on top of the list to monitor and manage the distribution grid. In this context, the EU project *Net2DG*, [4] proposes a solution in terms of an ICT infrastructure based software that enables smart grid applications to function on top of a set of aggregated data sources. As a part of *Net2DG* project, two field tests: one in Denmark and one in Germany, and a laboratory setup has been setup and used to demonstrate feasibility of using ICT in context of executing several different useful smart grid applications. This paper presents the main aspects, results and experiences of the Danish field test.

Keywords: Smart grids · Grid observability · Distribution grids · Advanced Metering Infrastructure

1 Background and Motivation

The latest political trends in Denmark points towards a high increase of renewable energy, electric vehicles, heat pumps and other, [1,3], which relies heavily on the low voltage distribution grid. At the same time, the DSO's are not fully aware of the state at this level, meaning that load, congestion and voltage levels are only under consideration when problems arises. This is not sustainable in the longer time horizon, and either grid reinforcement is required which is estimated to around 5–6 billion DKR per year, just to support the expected amounts of electrical vehicles in DK, [2]. Alternative to this investment cost is smart IT based solution for monitoring and management of the distribution grid.

In this light, the EU project *Net2DG*, [4] has been addressing this issue by developing ICT infrastructure solution to enable smart grid applications to function on top of a set of aggregated data sources. As a part of *Net2DG* project, two field tests: one in Denmark and one in Germany, and a laboratory setup has been setup and used to demonstrate feasibility of using ICT in different technical context. These smart grid applications include not only the grid observability

---

Thanks to the consortium of the EU project Net2DG for their support for this paper.

R. Adler et al. (Eds.): EDCC 2021 Workshops, CCIS 1462, pp. 82–89, 2021.
https://doi.org/10.1007/978-3-030-86507-8_8

applications such as grid monitoring, loss calculation, outage detection and diagnosis etc. but also the control applications such as automatic voltage control. In this paper we present the main aspects of one of this field test, namely the Danish one. In this context, we present the results and experiences of the field test, while for completeness Table 1 gives an overview of the complementary and synergies within the three instruments of assessment.

Table 1. Overview of complementary and synergies for the two field test and laboratory in *Net2DG* [6].

	Complementarities	Synergies
Thy-Mors energy	Interoperability with AMI and Solarweb Head End System	Provides data input and parameters for digital assessment framework
	Validation of software under realistic conditions	Scenario with measurement at customer site (Smart Meters)
Stw.Landau	Interoperability with SolarWeb and RTU Headend system	Provides data input and parameters for digital assessment framework
	Validation of software under realistic conditions	Scenario with measurements at junction boxes
Digital assessment framework	Validation of software under extreme operational scenarios	Allows sensitivity analysis for erroneous data
	Extensive sensitivity analysis	Provides guidelines for field test executions
	Repetitive tests for statistical analysis of application performance	Provides additional data for statistical analysis and confidences for result

In [7] a set of user stories where defined to clarify the use of the system. Some of the most relevant to the Danish case are:

- Post Outage diagnostics: detection and diagnostics of outage to reduce the time to correct power failures
- Voltage quality monitoring: in order to validate that the voltage supply quality is acceptable or not
- Reduce losses in the distribution grid: to reduce OPEX of the distribution grid.

To support these user stories, and their related use cases, the Net2DG system architecture is required to provide the relevant data and interfaces which are described in Sect. 2.

2   System Architecture

The IT architecture for the system deployed in the field test is illustrated in Fig. 1, [8], and is responsible for the fusion and mapping of measurements to the grid topology as well as other related functionalities. This architecture shows four main blocks: the Application Layer, the ICT Gateway (along with a Data Base), the headend layer with different headends (AMI, SolarWeb and Grid topology) and a Graphical User Interface (GUI).

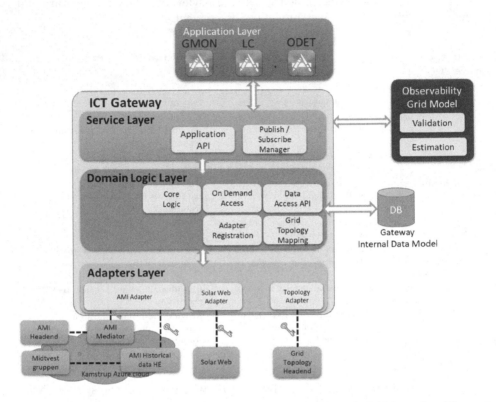

Fig. 1. Overview of the ICT-GW as deployed in the Danish field test site, [6].

The **Application Layer** includes novel applications developed in the context of the *Net2DG* project aiming at supporting the DSO in three main areas: (1) Operation Efficiency, (2) Voltage Quality and (3) Outage Diagnosis. Each of the application runs on top of the ICT Gateway (ICT-GW) and retrieves the grid topology information, the measurements and the events through the IC-GW.

The **ICT-GW** is in charge of establishing connections to the different data and actuation subsystems, in addition to the Grid Topology Subsystem, which is in charge to provide the topological information of the electrical grid under observation. Due to heterogeneity of subsystems deployed in the field, the ICT-GW needs to adapt the collected data in a uniform format to be easily stored in the Data Base and to be provided to the applications that will request them. The ICT-GW comrises of three different layers i.e. (1) Service Layer, (2) Domain Logic Layer and (3) the Adapters Layer. A brief description of these layers is presented below:

1. The **Service Layer** provides the application program interface (API) to the application as well as observability grid model (OGM) and manages the publish/subscriptions aspect of the application interaction with the ICT-GW. The OGM block calculates missing electrical parameters for the grid observability applications (e.g., calculate voltage values for all grid nodes in the LV topology). Moreover, the OGM is also used to calculate the cable loading for cables and lines.
2. The **Domain Logic** contains functionality to ensure topology mapping, data normalization, access control to actuation units, security and resilience functionality and in general core logic to mediate application demands with information supply at the subsystem level.
3. The **Adapter Layer** ensures that subsystem information access and flow is available to the ICT-GW and enables the interfacing to the subsystems. Each adapter is therefore specifically tailored to a given subsystem of a specific vendor or provider. In the following we detail the deployment scenario and the various subsystems and their characteristics.

In order to allow the users, namely the DSO operators, to interact with the *Net2DG* system, the GUI has been designed and developed to provide input to both the ICT-GW and the applications and to receive output from them.

2.1   Field Trial Deployment

This field trial is located in North-Western Denmark and consists of a complete secondary substation providing power supply to a small village. There are 98 customers (household, small industry, public institutions, supermarket, etc.) connected to five low voltage feeders. There are several roof-top solar PV installations and there is a 100% roll-out of smart meters in the area. Figure 2 shows an overview of the Danish field trial deployment.

The characteristic part of this field test is the use of the cloud environment to host interface components at the adapter layer. This enables scaling up/down computational resources as at deployment stage this is only estimated, see [8]. Figure 2 also reveals to some degree, the complexity that exists in the integration of different data sources, and its related support systems to develop and perform pre-tests.

2.2   Access to Advanced Metering Infrastructure (AMI)

The AMI adapter has to main functionalities to support i.e. 1) to provide access to historical data, and 2) to provide on-demand access to smart meters. The AMI Adapter in the field setups is challenged by a set of strong security layers in the AMI data collection subsystem. As a solution an Azure cloud has been established as an intermediate zone, in which Net2DG has installed relevant software that links to the ICT-GW. The two functionalities requires two very different technical interfaces to the AMI system, so these have been split into separate Head-End systems, one for historical data and one for on-demand access.

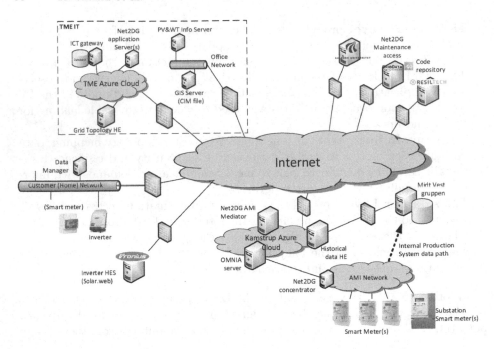

Fig. 2. Overview of the ICT-GW and related subsystems integrated in the Danish field test [5].

The historical data access expects data to be pushed to a particular location every 6 h, from where it fetches the latest update containing measurements and events within the last 6 h period. The files requires parsing and is after that pushed to the ICT-GW.

To allow the on-demand access, a separate concentrator has been setup in the field to not disturb the running production system. Any failure of that, will have financial consequences for the DSO. A *Net2DG* mediator has been inserted to establish the interface between the AMI direct access and the ICT-GW via a separate adapter. The solution allows a REST based API to the ICT-GW which ensures the required flexibility of the interface.

2.3 Access to PV Inverters

In the field test area there is only remote access to one PV unit, but that one offers both set point changes as well as readings with 5 min intervals, which is located near already installed smart meter, offering a higher time granularity measurement. The inverter access is done via a web interface called SolarWeb. The ICT-GW needs for this data source then to align sampling time such that measurements between the AMI and PV Inverter may be used in conjunction to each other. Although not installed at this point in time, synchronization across the subsystem will be required as each data provider potentially have their individual time synchronization system. More generically, the ICT-GW must ensure that output from this and the AMI subsystem is aligned in terms of metadata.

2.4   Access to Grid Topology

The grid topology used for the field test is exported from a database into an XML file using the CIM model. This subsystem requires significant parsing, and some details have been detailed in [9, 10], whereas the internal structure of the Grid Topology Headend is shown in Fig. 3.

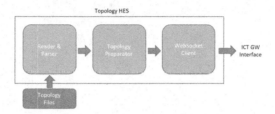

Fig. 3. Grid Topology Headend subsystem for the Danish field test [5].

The critical element with this subsystem is that the topology is parsed correctly, and that the file itself represents correctly the grid. Since the generation of this file, at some point in the process, requires human translation between notes from the installation crew and the database, it is however, most likely that it includes some minor errors. Therefore, the ICT-GW must support functionality to validate also the grid topology by making use of measurements. This, however, is a part of the next steps. The current input file format support for the Danish field test is the CIM-XML model, [5], which may also need to be extended to support other formats.

3   Assessment, Validation and Learnings

One of the most critical applications that is objective to the Danish field test, is grid monitoring as shown in Fig. 1, which includes functionality to correctly show and map relevant measurement to the operator. An example of GUI is shown in Fig. 4.

From this GUI, the operator is able to click on each smart meter and substation (red triangle), and start application that generate several analysis. Figure 5 shows a case where the substation has been selected. What is seen here is the lumped voltage over time, including lower and upper 10% quantiles to indicate the spread of the voltage also as a function of time.

More statistics of different metrics, e.g. frequency, load, reactive power analysis, can also be done via the screen. Hereby enabling the DSO to operate their grids as intended in Sect. 1.

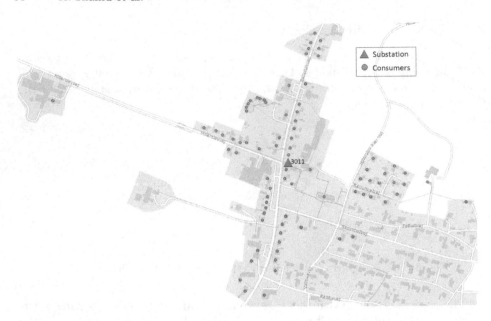

Fig. 4. Screenshot of GUI from the Danish field test case showing locations of smart meters, [6].

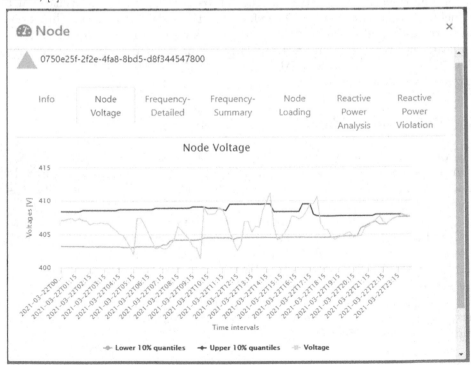

Fig. 5. Screenshot of GUI from the Danish field test case showing locations of smart meters, [6].

4   Conclusions and Outlook

The experiences and learning's from the field test in Denmark has been on both technical and non-technical levels. Clearly there are challenges in integrating data from various sources, but the critical part is related to 1) the input data quality as well as 2) the mapping between different providers and the grid topology provided by the DSO. If just one of those fails, then output of the system can easily be questionable as well. In the next steps, the focus will be on how to ensure high quality output to applications, despite low quality input by utilizing multiple data input sources.

Acknowledgment. The research leading to these results has received funding from the European Union's Horizon 2020 research and innovation programme under grant agreement No 774145 for the Net2DG Project (www.net2dg.eu).

References

1. Danish Energy Association: Smart distribution grids power Europe's transition to green energy. state of green, March 2017. https://www.danskenergi.dk/sites/danskenergi.dk/files/media/dokumenter/2017-11/DSO_Magazine_210x297_ENG_V10.pdf
2. Dansk energi: Elbilerne kommer - det er et politisk valg hvordan vi sikrer at elnettet bliver klart. dansk energi, May 2019. https://www.danskenergi.dk/sites/danskenergi.dk/files/media/dokumenter/2019-05/Elbilerne_kommer_gor_elnettet_klart_til_elbilerne.pdf
3. Dansk energi: Elnet til fremtiden - og fortsat i verdensklasse. elnet-outlook, oktober 2018. https://www.danskenergi.dk/sites/danskenergi.dk/files/media/dokumenter/2018-10/ELNET_Outlook_2018_.pdf
4. Leveraging networked data for the digital electricity grid (Net2DG), grant agreement NR. 774145. http://www.net2dg.eu/
5. Iov, F., et al.: Net2DG deliverable D5.1 - first integrated deployment at lab and testbed and preliminary results. Technical report (2019)
6. Iov, F., et al.: Net2DG deliverable D5.3 - final consolidated results. Technical report (2021)
7. Schwefel, H.P., et al.: Net2DG deliverable D1.2 - initial baseline architecture. Technical report (2018)
8. Schwefel, H.P., et al.: Net2DG deliverable D3.1 - ICT analysis and gateway design. Technical report (2018)
9. Shahid, K., Schiavone, E., Drenjanac, D., Bæklund, R.P., Olsen, R.L., Schwefel, H.: Extraction of CIM-based distribution grid topology information for observability. In: 2019 15th European Dependable Computing Conference (EDCC), pp. 165–170 (2019)
10. Shahid, K., Schiavone, E., Drenjanac, D., Lyhne, M., Olsen, R.L., Schwefel, H.: Handling incomplete and erroneous grid topology information for low voltage grid observability. In: 2019 IEEE International Conference on Communications, Control, and Computing Technologies for Smart Grids (SmartGridComm), pp. 1–6 (2019)

Increased Renewable Hosting Capacity of a Real Low-Voltage Grid Based on Continuous Measurements – Results from an Actual PV Connection Request

Christine Schäler[1]([✉]), Klaus Strasser[1], Robert Damböck[2], and Hans-Peter Schwefel[1,3]

[1] GridData GmbH, Maximilianstrasse 33, 83278 Traunstein, Germany
`{schaeler,strasser,schwefel}@griddata.eu`
[2] Stadtwerke Landau a.d. Isar, Maria-Ward-Platz 1, 94405 Landau a.d. Isar, Germany
`Robert.Damboeck@stadtwerke.landau-isar.de`
[3] Aalborg University, 9220 Aalborg, Denmark

Abstract. The distributed generation and new load patterns caused by the energy transition put strong requirements on the distribution grids. The traditional worst-case planning approaches in the low-voltage grid will lead to excessive grid extensions. In this paper, through a digital twin of the low-voltage grid, the true status of the physical grid is used to detect grid bottlenecks and therefore allows to match grid investments to actual needs in the distribution grid. This paper presents preliminary results from a real case study for the novel planning approach which lead to an accurate picture of grid hosting capacity, which is a major step forward from previously used worst case assumptions.

Keywords: Low-voltage grid · Hosting capacity · Digital twin · Grid measurements

1 Introduction

The PV hosting capacity is the maximum amount of PV that can be added to a distribution grid before the distribution system operator (DSO) needs to upgrade resources like transformers or cables [6, 7]. Knowing the hosting capacity is essential for successful and resource-efficient grid operation. Currently, the industry-standard to determine hosting capacity [8] is a rudimentary baseline method that performs a simplified grid calculation for the worst-case where all PVs generate with peak power and no consumption is present. In a current real-world scenario at Stadtwerke Landau an der Isar, this worst-case planning method required to exchange the transformer as the total PV capacity installed was exceeding the total transformer capacity. In this paper, we propose a grid planning approach that is based on measurement data and on a digital twin that performs a load-flow analysis to derive non-measured voltages and cable and transformer loadings. The analysis of the historical measurements showed in the given usage scenario, that the transformer loading was not in a critical state during the last year of operation where a

© Springer Nature Switzerland AG 2021
R. Adler et al. (Eds.): EDCC 2021 Workshops, CCIS 1462, pp. 90–98, 2021.
https://doi.org/10.1007/978-3-030-86507-8_9

maximum loading of 70% was identified, and that true voltages in operation were quite far from the violation limits. Performing the proposed grid planning based on the digital twin showed a strongly increased hosting capacity. Consequently, the DSO did not have to replace the transformer and cabling. A subsequent continuous monitoring of the grid allows to automatically identify when a new situation arises from significantly changing loading patterns, as e.g., caused by the increased presence of electrical vehicle charging.

2 Field Trial Setup and PV Connection Case

The case study in this paper is based on a low voltage grid of the Stadtwerke in Landau and der Iar (StwLan) in Germany. In this section, we first describe the architecture of this grid. Second, we describe the digital twin built up for this study. Third, we present the PV connection request of the DSO the case study in this paper is driven by, together with the baseline method currently used in industry to assess this request.

2.1 Field Trial Architecture: Topology and Measurement Points

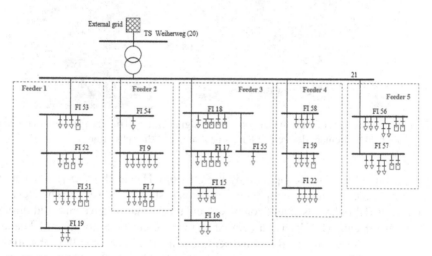

Fig. 1. Field trial low-voltage grid containing a 250 kVA secondary substation serving 5 feeders with loads (triangles) and significant PV generation (rectangles).

Figure 1 shows the low-voltage field trial area from StwLan. It consists of 28 PV systems (rectangles) with a total capacity of 270.573 kWp (78.14 kWp in Feeder 1), 78 customer connection boxes (triangles) representing customers and small businesses, junction boxes and a secondary substation with a 250 kVA transformer. This substation has 5 feeders, which are visualized in Fig. 1. In addition, there are two more feeders that are supplying power to streetlights not shown in the figure.

2.2 Digital Twin and Grid Monitoring Solution

To link the grid topology and measurements, in context of the Net2DG project (www.net 2dg.eu), a digital twin [1–3, 9] was built up. This digital twin is built up automatically through the grid topology data and heterogeneous measurements as shown in Fig. 2: (1) The ICT Gateway responsible for data fusion, (2) Headend Servers responsible for topology and measurement data collection, (3) the observability grid model (OGM) that implements a load flow analysis to calculate non-measured voltages and currents, and (4) applications to monitor the grid and support the digital planning process proposed in this paper based on the digital twin.

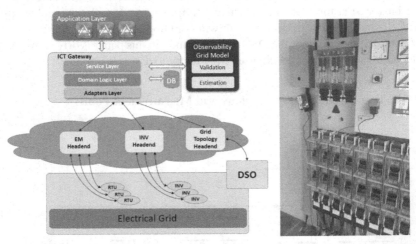

Fig. 2. Left: Architecture of the system to obtain the digital twin and run the planning application [1–3, 9]. Right: Measurement device and RTU installations at the substation.

The grid topology data is imported by the topology Headend server [5] by parsing an export from the existing geographic information system (GIS) server. The electrical measurements (EM) devices at junction boxes and the substation are connected through remote terminal units (RTUs) via a cellular network connection to the EM headend Server [10]. The RTUs are based on Raspberry Pis, the deployment in the substation is illustrated in Fig. 2 right. Technical details are described in [3]. Two PV inverters have been connected to the Fronius Solar.web portal (solarweb.com). The Inverter (INV) headend connects to Solar.web. In this study, we use measurements from the substation and one inverter. All subsystems are connected via secure VPN tunnels.

2.3 PV Connection Request and Baseline Method

The case study in this paper is based on a DSO request as follows: A new PV system with the size of 19.8 kWp should be added at junction box FI19 located in Feeder 1 (see Fig. 1). The question is whether the additional connection of this PV system exeeds the resource limitations, which are given by: (1) the transformer loadings, (2) the voltages at the customer connection boxes, and (3) the cable loadings.

The baseline method [8] currently used in industry to answer this question is a worst-case analysis: Assessing the existing infrastructure considering a pure infeed PV power production. The result is that the Trafo is already overloaded with a load of 270.573/250 = 108.2%. Consequently, Feeder 1 can only carry a total of 78 kWp PV and no additional PV injection is possible. Limiting resources were the loading of the transformer, and the voltage rise calculated by the worst-case planning approach. Consequently, the worst-case planning method required to exchange the transformer. Furthermore, the worst case planning also showed a too high voltage increase and therefore would required cable replacements or additional cabling.

Since this method does not use any measurement data, the worst-case analysis provides a simplified and rudimentary approach for defining the PV hosting capacity.

3 Planning Based on a Digital Twin with Real Measurement Data

The baseline method does not use any measurement data and is therefore rudimentary. In this section, we therefore propose a grid planning approach based on measurement data, that provides realistic results and prevents the DSO from not required purchases and therefore, ultimately, saves costs. To this end, we first present the approach, second present a case study based on this approach, and third discuss the results of the case study and relate them to the baseline worst-case method.

3.1 Grid Planning Approach

In this section, we describe the used measurement data, performed data preprocessing as well as calculation of grid parameters of our approach. To determine the maximum hosting capacity, the grid planning approach is generally executed multiple times for different loading scenarios.

Input Measurement Data. To investigate the request by the DSO, the 15 min. measurement data of only two measurement points available in the digital twin was required to achieve good accuracy:

1) Substation Transformer: Voltage V^{Trafo} as well as active P^{Trafo} and reactive Q^{Trafo} power.
2) Reference PV system: Measurements of a reference PV power production profile to model the individual PV systems installed in Feeder 1. A power factor of 1.0 is assumed for all PV systems.

Measurement Data Preprocessing. The approach involved the following steps, implemented by a digital planning application on top of the digital twin. Let T be period considered time interval.

1) Obtain the historic worst case of voltage measurements in V^{Trafo}:

$$\text{historic worst case } V_{Max}^{Trafo} = \max_{t \in T} V^{Trafo}[t]$$

where $V^{Trafo}[t]$ is the voltage measurement at time t.

2) Use the reference PV system to extrapolate the generation P^{PVi} of each PV plant PV_i by scaling it with the peak power ratio.

3) For each time stamp t in T, sum up all PV generation to obtain the total generation in the low-voltage grid area:

$$\text{Sum of all PV profiles at time t } = \sum\nolimits_{PVi} P^{PVi}[t]$$

4) Correct the measurements P^{Trafo} and Q^{Trafo} by removing the generation to obtain the total consumption in the grid:

$$\text{Sum of all loads at time t } = P^{Trafo} - \text{sum of all PV profiles at time t.}$$

5) Equally distribute the total consumption over all loads connected to the LV grid area:

$$P^{CCBi}[t] = \text{Sum of all loads at time t/number of all CCBS}$$

In the used case-study, there were no larger industrial loads in the LV grid area. However, the information about the special types of consumers can also be included for a proportional and time-of-day dependent splitting of the total load across all CCBs in the LV grid area.

Calculation of Grid Parameters. Based on the obtained consumption and generation profiles and the historic worst-case voltage V_{Max}^{Trafo} at the substation, the digital twin uses the observability grid model OGM to calculate the following: the currents I_δ^{ci} of all cables c_i, the P_δ^{Trafo} and Q_δ^{Trafo} at the substation, and voltages V_δ^{CCBi} at all customer connection boxes after adding an additional PV generation of δ kW. Based on this, it outputs the following parameters and compares them with relevant violation thresholds:

(1) Transformer loadings: $\text{LoadTrafo}[t] = \dfrac{\sqrt{(P_\delta^{Trafo}[t])^2 + (Q_\delta^{Trafo}[t])^2}}{\text{Transformer capacity}} \leq 90\%$

(2) Cable loading for all cables c_i: $\text{Load } c_i[t] = \dfrac{I_\delta^{ci}}{\text{capacity of } c_i} \leq 90\%$

(3) Voltage V_δ^{CCBi} at all customer connection boxes ≤ 440 V.

The hosting capacity of the grid is the PV capacity so far plus the maximum δ with that the conditions (1)–(3) are fulfilled.

3.2 Performance of Case Study

We used the proposed grid planning approach for our case study. Before we describe the results in Sect. 3.3, we describe in this section how the used input measurement data, preprocessing and iteration steps looked like in this study.

Input Measurement Data. The grid planning approach proposed in Sect. 3.1 was implemented as a new application and used to assess the grid integration of a new PV system at junction box FI 19 in StwLan field trial. The study was performed on the measurement data of one spring week with maximum PV generation of the reference PV. Figure 3 shows the extrapolated PV generation and calculated total loads (red curve) as well as the active power P^{Trafo} (yellow) in this week.

Measurement Data Preprocessing. To calculate the historic worst case, we used voltage measurements in the period from August 2020 to April 2021. The result is

$$\text{Historic worst case } V_{Max}^{Trafo} = \max_{t \in T} V^{Trafo}[t] = 410.6 \, V.$$

Iterative Calculation of Grid Parameters. To determine the maximum hosting capacity, the grid planning approach is executed multiple times for different loading scenarios. Specifically, the planning application incrementally connected PV systems in 3 kWp (i.e., $\delta = 3,6,..$) steps at all existing CCBs in Feeder 1 in a round-robin fashion.

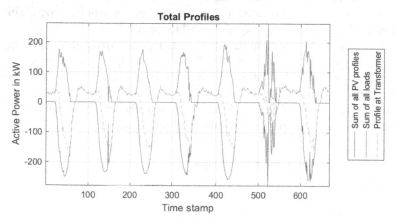

Fig. 3. Approach to determine load and generation profiles.

3.3 Summary of Results

Table 1 states a summary of the results achieved in the study, which are as follows.

First, one can connect to 102 kWp in Feeder 1 before one violates the voltage limitations at the CCBs. Figure 4 shows the voltages at all customer connection boxes in this case: The limit of 10% over nominal is reached. However, at this stage, the loading of the transformer and the cables are with maximum 64.9% far below the limit of 90%. Observe that this is already 24 kWp more than determined by the baseline. This means for the concrete DSO request described in Sect. 2.3, that the additional 19.8 kWp PV system can be added without violating voltage or loading limits.

Table 1. Summary of PV hosting capacity results for the field-trial Feeder 1.

Approach	Main Constraints on Resources	Other Constraints on Resources	PV hosting cap. Feeder 1	Increase to baseline
Baseline	*Tranfo load > 108%*	*Cable loading*	*78 kWp*	*Baseline*
Grid Planning	Voltage at CCBs ≤ 440 V	Trafo load ≤ 64.9% Cable load ≤ 34.9%	102 kWp	**31%**
Grid Planning	Trafo Loading ≤ 90%	Cable load ≤ 77%	201 kWp	**158%**
Grid Planning	Cable Loading ≤ 90%		234 kWp	**200%**

Second, if one can tackle voltage violations at the CCBs, one can connect PV systems with up to 201 kWp before reaching the transformer load limit. Figure 5 illustrates the transformer loading with additionally 123 kWp PV connected at Feeder 1 assessed for seven days. As shown, the 90% loading limit is reached, but not exceeded. This is an increase of 158% of hosting capacity compared to the baseline.

Third, in case one then again accepts violating the Transformer loading limit (because, e.g., one accepts to replace this Trafo with a bigger one), one is even able to connect PV systems with total 234 kWp. This is an increase of 200% of hosting capacity compared to the baseline.

Therefore, there is a substantial benefit of using the proposed approach that is supported by historic measurement data and load flow analysis.

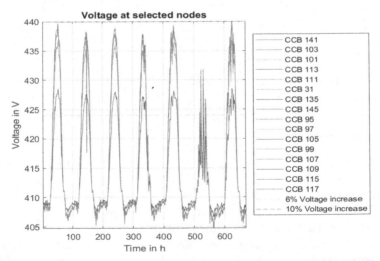

Fig. 4. Voltage at nodes with additional 24 kWp PV installations distributed in Feeder 1.

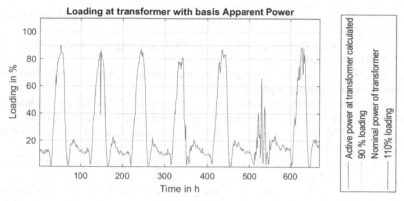

Fig. 5. Transformer loading with additionally 123 kWp PV capacity in Feeder 1.

4   Discussion and Outlook

The maximum hosting capacity of a grid is an important variable for a DSO to know whether he needs to buy new transformers and cables with higher capacity in case new PV systems should be connected. This paper proposes a grid planning approach that determines the maximum hosting capacity of a distribution grid by using a digital twin. Compared to the currently used rudimentary baseline method, the digital twin allows to use measurement data and load flow analysis in the grid planning approach. To evaluate the approach, a case study with a real German was performed. The study proves that the proposed grid planning approach reveals that the actual hosting capacity is up to 200% higher than determined by the baseline. Compared to the baseline method, using the proposed grid planning approach saves cost for the DSO, as it prevents him from buying new transformers and cables if there is no need.

As future work, we aim at investigating how inaccurate measurements, e.g., due to measurement errors or data perturbation [11, 12] influence the grid planning results.

Acknowledgments. This work was supported by the European Union's Horizon 2020 research and innovation program under grant agreement No 774145 within the project Net2DG. The authors would like to thank all project partners for their feedback and input. The results of this work have been summarized in a project Deliverable [4].

References

1. Handrup, K. (ed.): Net2DG Deliverable D1.2 – Initial Baseline Architecture, August 2019
2. Nostro, N. (ed.): Net2DG Deliverable D3.1 - ICT Analysis and Gateway Design, December 2018
3. Iov, F. (ed.): Net2DG Deliverable D5.1 - First integrated deployment at Lab and Testbed and preliminary results, December 2019
4. Iov, F. (ed.): Net2DG Deliverable D5.3 – Final consolidated results, June 2021
5. Shahid, K., et al.: Handling incomplete and erroneous grid topology information for low voltage grid observability. In: 2019 IEEE SmartGridComm. IEEE (2019)

6. Samar, F., et al.: Review on the PV hosting capacity in distribution networks. Energies MDPI **13**, 4756 (2020)
7. Laaksonen, H., et al.: Technologies to increase PV hosting capacity in distribution feeders. In: PESGM. IEEE (2016)
8. Damböck, R.: Einspeiseberechnungsprogramm. VeBW Seminar Netzberechnung für Energieerzeugungsanlagen Nürnberg
9. Nainar, K., et al.: Experimental validation and deployment of observability applications for monitoring of low-voltage distribution grids. In: Sensors. MDPI (2021, to appear)
10. Nostro, N., et al.: Resilient access to heterogeneous measurement data for grid observability. In: EDCC. IEEE (2019)
11. Tex, C., et al.: PrivEnergy: A Privacy Operator Framework Addressing Individual Concerns. E-Energy. ACM (2018)
12. Tex, C., et al.: Swellfish Privacy: Exploiting Time-Dependent Relevance for Continuous Differential Privacy. KIT Scientific Working Papers (2020)

Workshop on Software Engineering
for Resilient Systems (SERENE)

International Workshop on Software Engineering for Resilient Systems (SERENE)

Workshop Description

SERENE 2021 is the 13th International Workshop on Software Engineering for Resilient Systems, held as a satellite event of the European Dependable Computing Conference (EDCC).

Resilient systems avoid, withstand, recover from, adapt, and evolve to handle anticipated and unforeseen disruptions, i.e., changes, faults, failure, and adversity. Resilience is particularly relevant for modern software and software-controlled systems that must continually adapt their architecture and parameters in response to evolving requirements, customer feedback, new business needs, and platform upgrades. Furthermore, given that software systems may provide critical services to society, e.g., in transportation, healthcare, energy production and e-government, it is paramount they continue to function correctly and reliably despite disruptions. Therefore, design for resilience is an increasingly important area of software engineering.

The SERENE workshop aims to bring together leading researchers and practitioners from academia and industry to advance state of the art and identify open challenges for engineering resilient software systems.

This year, five papers were submitted. Three members of the Program Committee reviewed each submission, and five papers were accepted for presentation.

The format of the workshop includes a keynote on socio-technical resilience delivered by the eminent Prof. Bashar Nuseibeh followed by technical sessions for presenting the papers.

We would like to thank the SERENE Steering Committee and the SERENE 2021 Program Committee, who made the workshop possible. We would also like to thank EDCC for hosting our workshop, the EDCC workshop chair Ilir Gashi, the EDCC publication chair André Martin for their help and support, and the editors of CCIS Springer who accepted the papers for publication. The EasyChair system facilitated the logistics of our job as Program Chairs. And above all, we sincerely thank the authors for their research efforts; their excellent contributions are what make this workshop possible.

Automated Generation of Configurable Cloud-Native Chaos Testbeds

Jacopo Soldani[(✉)] and Antonio Brogi

Department of Computer Science, University of Pisa, Pisa, Italy
{jacopo.soldani,antonio.brogi}@unipi.it

Abstract. We propose CHAOS ECHO, a framework for automatically generating configurable testbeds that can be exploited to assess techniques enhancing cloud-native applications with fault resilience mechanisms, like orchestrators recovering failed services, or failure detection and root cause analysis techniques. The testbeds generated by CHAOS ECHO feature chaos testing out-of-the-box, and they can be configured to vary the topology of target applications or the configuration of their services, like the rates of failures and service interactions.

Keywords: Chaos testing · Fault resilience · Cloud-native application

1 Introduction

Cloud-native applications, like microservices, became the de-facto standard for delivering enterprise IT applications [3]. At the same time, cloud-native applications often include hundreds of interacting services, and this makes it harder to monitor the application services to detect whether they have failed, or whether the failure in a service was due to a cascade of failures of other services. It is hence crucial to ensure fault resilience of the services forming a cloud-native application, e.g., by operating them with orchestrators capable of recovering services from failures, or by determining the root causes for a failure on a service to intervene and avoid such failure to happen again [7].

After Netflix's Chaos Monkey [5], chaos testing became one of the most used approaches to assess the fault resilience of cloud-native applications themselves. Chaos testing consists in proactively simulating and identifying failures in an application before their actual occurrence can lead to unplanned downtime or a negative user experience. Netflix's Chaos Monkey follows this idea by randomly injecting failures in application services to check whether such services can actually recover from injected failures. The same approach is followed by currently existing alternatives to Netflix's Chaos Monkey, e.g., Pumba [4] or ChaosBlade [2]. Such an approach allows IT and DevOps teams to quickly identify and resolve issues due to failures from which an application cannot recover [1].

Inspired by chaos testing [1], we propose a novel approach to tackle an orthogonal problem, viz., assessing the performance of techniques devised to enforce fault resilience in cloud-native applications (rather than assessing the fault resilience of

R. Adler et al. (Eds.): EDCC 2021 Workshops, CCIS 1462, pp. 101–108, 2021.
https://doi.org/10.1007/978-3-030-86507-8_10

cloud-native applications themselves). We indeed propose CHAOS ECHO, a framework for automatically generating configurable testbed applications, which run multiple interacting CHAOS ECHO SERVICEs, each simulating the possible interactions and failures of a service in a cloud-native application. CHAOS ECHO enables users to specify (a) the topology of the desired testbed application, viz., number of CHAOS ECHO SERVICEs to run and their dependencies, and (b) the configuration of each CHAOS ECHO SERVICE therein, viz., how many replicas of a service to run, its probability of invoking the services it depends on, and its probabilities of failing to process a request or to suddenly "crash" and stop responding to its clients. Given one such specification, the CHAOS ECHO COMPOSER automatically generates a testbed application, which can then be run with Docker, the de-facto standard for container orchestration in cloud [6].

Obtained testbed applications, triggered by the CHAOS ECHO WORKLOAD GENERATOR, can then be directly exploited to assess the performance of techniques devised for enforcing fault resilience in cloud-native applications, e.g., orchestrators capable of recovering failed services, or techniques for detecting failures in services or identifying their possible root causes. Obtained applications indeed feature chaos testing out-of-the-box, they can be configured to vary their topology and the configuration of their services, and the WORKLOAD GENERATOR can also be configured to vary the workload for a testbed application. This enables assessing techniques for enhancing fault resilience under varying configurations and workload of obtained testbed applications. We showcase this by illustrating how CHAOS ECHO can be used to analyze Docker Swarm's performance in recovering failed services, when increasing the failure rates of services or horizontally scaling them to obtain multiple running instances of each service.

To the best of our knowledge, ours is the first framework enabling to generate configurable testbed applications for assessing techniques enforcing cloud-native applications' fault resilience. Such assessment is indeed currently done by injecting failures (either manually or through tools à la Chaos Monkey) in existing applications (e.g., Sock Shop [9] or TrainTicket [10]) to evaluate whether, e.g., an orchestrator can effectively recover failing services, whether injected failures are detected, or whether their root causes are identified [7]. The topology and configuration of existing applications are however fixed, hence making it harder to evaluate newly proposed techniques over varying application topologies and running configurations [7], which is precisely what CHAOS ECHO supports.

2   Specifying Testbed Applications

We hereby illustrate how users can specify a desired testbed application by simply indicating its topology and the configuration the SERVICEs therein.

Testbed Application Specification. Testbed applications can be structured according to any desired topology, by simply indicating the `services` forming the application and how each service `depends_on` other services. For instance, Fig. 1 specifies a three-tiered application, viz., a `frontend` depending on a `backend`, which in turn depends on a `database`.

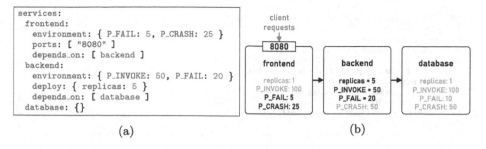

Fig. 1. Example of (a) input application specification and (b) graphical representation of the corresponding testbed application. In (b), boxes denote the specified SERVICES and their configuration (with light grey denoting the default configuration values assigned to the parameters not specified in (a)), whilst arrows denote service interactions.

The `services` can also be configured to differentiate their runtime behaviour. Their rates of service interactions and failures can indeed be configured by setting the `environment` variables P_INVOKE, P_FAIL, and P_CRASH. The desired number of `replicas` of each service can also be specified, as well as whether the possibly multiple instances of a service can be reached by external clients on given `ports`. As shown in Fig. 1, the configuration is optional for a service (e.g., `database` fully rely on default values), and it can possibly differ from service to service (e.g., `frontend` and `backend` are configured with different values for P_FAIL).

It is worth highlighting how `depends_on`, P_INVOKE, P_FAIL, and P_CRASH enable customising the behaviour of each CHAOS ECHO SERVICE in an application specification. If no service is included in `depends_on`, a CHAOS ECHO SERVICE will simulate the behaviour of services that directly reply to requests received from other services in cloud-native applications, e.g., databases or message queues, hence never invoking other services to process an incoming request. Instead, if there are services on which a CHAOS ECHO SERVICE `depends_on`, the latter will invoke such services while processing a request. The SERVICE will hence simulate the behaviour of services actively invoking other services to process their incoming requests, e.g., gateways and frontend/internal services. In this case, the probability of invoking each backend service is determined by P_INVOKE. A P_INVOKE set to 1 results in all the services in `depends_on` always being invoked, whilst smaller values result in random subsets of such services being invoked. P_FAIL and P_CRASH instead enable controlling the failure proneness of each CHAOS ECHO SERVICE. They indeed enable setting the probability of a CHAOS ECHO SERVICE failing in processing an incoming request and that of crashing when a failure occurs, respectively. To better illustrate how `depends_on`, P_INVOKE, P_FAIL, and P_CRASH enables customising the behaviour of a CHAOS ECHO SERVICE, we now illustrate how CHAOS ECHO SERVICES work.

How Chaos Echo Services Work. A service in a cloud-native application may receive requests from external clients or from other internal services, and it may invoke other services to process such requests. A CHAOS ECHO SERVICE simulates

```
PROCESS(m, depends_on, P_INVOKE, P_FAIL, P_CRASH):
1    status ← 200
2    for s ∈ depends_on
3        with probability P_INVOKE do
4            ⟨m', status'⟩ ← INVOKE(s, randomMessage)
5            if status' ≠ 200 then status ← 500
6    with probability P_FAIL do
7        with probability P_CRASH do exit
8        status ← 500
9    if status ≠ 200 then m ← errorMessage
10   REPLY(m, status)
```

Fig. 2. CHAOS ECHO SERVICE behaviour.

this behaviour, while at the same time simulating the possibility for a service to fail while processing an incoming request. Following chaos testing's principles [1], each SERVICE randomly select the backend services to invoke among those they are connected to, and its failures are also random.

A CHAOS ECHO SERVICE indeed processes each incoming request by running the PROCESS procedure in Fig. 2, where m denotes the message contained in such request, whilst depends_on, P_INVOKE, P_FAIL, and P_CRASH are configuration parameters for customising the service behaviour. If no error occurs while processing the incoming request (lines 2–9), the service echos the original message m with the HTTP *status* code set to 200 (lines 1 and 10). Instead, if some error occurred and caused the *status* code to differ from 200, an *errorMessage* is set to be returned to the client that sent the request under processing (line 9).

A CHAOS ECHO SERVICE can be configured to simulate the processing of an incoming request by invoking one or more services it depends on (viz., those in the list depends_on), with the latter intended to be CHAOS ECHO SERVICEs as well. If this is the case, each incoming request is processed by interacting with a random subset of the services in depends_on (lines 2–5), with the probability of invoking a service $s \in$ depends_on constrained by the parameter P_INVOKE (line 3). A *randomMessage* is sent to any invoked service s (line 4). If s replies with an error message, or if a timeout expires and *status'* remains unset, then the *status* code to be returned by the present service is set to 500. This enables simulating errors that occurred while processing the incoming request, due to the fact that some invoked service answered with an error or was unresponsive (line 5). Otherwise, the *status* code is left unchanged and the request processing continues.

A CHAOS ECHO SERVICE can also be configured to simulate internal failures while processing an incoming request, not due to failing interactions with invoked services (lines 6–8). The probability of failing is constrained by the parameter P_FAIL (line 6). If a failure is selected to occur, the CHAOS ECHO SERVICE simulates an unexpected crash with probability P_CRASH. This is done by suddenly closing the whole service, hence stopping to answer to any of its clients, therein included that sending the message m under processing (line 7). Otherwise, it sets the status code to 500 to simulate an internal error due to which it fails in processing the message m, whilst continuing to serve its clients (line 8).

Fig. 3. Deployment, load, and logging of multiple interacting CHAOS ECHO SERVICES.

3 Running Testbed Applications

The process for generating, deploying, and loading a testbed application running multiple CHAOS ECHO SERVICES is shown in Fig. 3. Given an input application specification, the COMPOSER automatically generates a Docker Compose file, which enables deploying multiple interacting CHAOS ECHO SERVICES, each in in its own Docker container. The Compose file also includes an ELK stack (viz., *Elasticsearch*, *Logstash*, and *Kibana*) to be deployed alongside the CHAOS ECHO SERVICES to enable storing and accessing all their logs. The obtained Docker Compose file can then be executed by an orchestrator, e.g., Docker Swarm [8], and loaded with the WORKLOAD GENERATOR.

After illustrating our implementation of the CHAOS ECHO SERVICES, we describe how the COMPOSER and the WORKLOAD GENERATOR can be used to generate, deploy, and load testbed applications. We also discuss how running testbed applications and accessing their logs enable assessing existing techniques for enhancing cloud-native applications' fault resilience.

Chaos Echo Services: Implementation. The CHAOS ECHO SERVICE is an open-source Spring Boot application,[1] whose Docker image is publicly available on the Docker Hub.[2] The application implements an HTTP API listening on port 80 and offering an endpoint/echo where to send POST requests. Each POST request is processed by a method implementing the pseudo-code in Fig. 2, which can be customised by setting the environment variables DEPENDS_ON, P_INVOKE, P_FAIL, and P_CRASH on the host where it runs (with their default values being the empty list, 100, 10, and 50, respectively). An additional environment variable (viz., TIMEOUT) allows setting the timeout in service interactions.

The application also logs events by exploiting the native Log4J support in Spring Boot. It logs all service interactions and the exchanged messages, with severity INFO if successful, while logging the reception of error messages from backend services with severity ERROR. It also logs the occurrence of all internal errors with severity ERROR, while it randomly decides whether to log "crashes" (still with severity ERROR). To anyhow ensure the logging of all failure events, "crashes" are always logged with severity DEBUG. This provides a sort of "ground truth", which can be useful, e.g., when evaluating techniques for analysing the logs generated by multiple interacting CHAOS ECHO SERVICES to detect anomalies or to determine the root causes for a failure [7].

---

[1] https://github.com/di-unipi-socc/chaos-echo.

[2] https://hub.docker.com/repository/docker/diunipisocc/chaosecho.

Generating, Deploying, and Loading Testbed Applications. Testbed application specifications (Sect. 2) can be processed with the COMPOSER[3] to obtain Docker Compose files, which can then be deployed with any Docker-compliant orchestrator (Fig. 3). Deployed applications can also be loaded by simulating end-requests, hence triggering interactions among the deployed instances of the CHAOS ECHO SERVICES. This can be done with the WORKLOAD GENERATOR, a bash script sending non-blocking CURL requests to a publicly accessible CHAOS ECHO SERVICE.[4] The WORKLOAD GENERATOR can also be configured by changing the address and port where to send requests, the period between requests, and the load duration, hence enabling to further customise the tests to run with a testbed application.

All events logged by the CHAOS ECHO SERVICES forming the deployed application are made accessible by the ELK stack deployed alongside such services. Logged events can indeed by browsed, at runtime, through *Kibana*'s web-based GUI. *Logstash* also dumps the logs in a file that is permanently stored on the file system so that it can be later accessed offline.

Assessing Techniques. The testbed applications generated with CHAOS ECHO enable assessing a technique for enhancing fault resilience of cloud-native applications against multiple different deployments of interacting CHAOS ECHO SERVICES, varying the application topology or the configuration of running services. The runtime behaviour of a testbed application can be observed through the web-based GUI offered by *Kibana* or through Docker native monitoring support. Both indeed enable observing whether a service failed, allowing, e.g., to assess whether a failure detection system effectively detected the failure of a service. In addition, they enable observing a service's status, allowing, e.g., to check whether an orchestrator successfully recovered a failed service.

Offline analyses can also be performed, thanks to the log dump produced by *Logstash* (Fig. 3). Logged events can be processed with root cause analysis techniques to assess their performance and accuracy in determining the possible root causes of observed failures. In addition, the timestamps associated with logged events can be used to measure, e.g., the performance of an orchestrator in recovering failing services, as we showcase in the following section.

4   Showcasing Chaos Echo

We hereafter report on a simple experiment we run to measure whether/how the recovery performance of Docker Swarm degrade under varying configurations of running applications. Notice that our objective here is only to showcase the use of CHAOS ECHO to generate configurable testbeds for assessing whether/how a technique succeeds in enforcing cloud-native applications' fault resilience. An exhaustive evaluation of Docker Swarm is outside of the scope of this paper.

---

[3] https://github.com/di-unipi-socc/chaos-echo-composer.
[4] https://github.com/di-unipi-socc/chaos-echo/blob/main/generate_workload.sh.

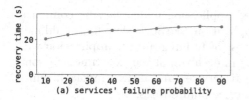 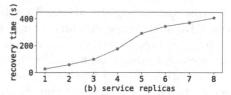

Fig. 4. Average time to recover failing instances of the CHAOS ECHO SERVICEs, under varying (a) service failure probability, viz., P_FAIL, and (b) number of service replicas.

In the experiment, we fixed the application topology by mirroring that of Sock Shop [9], viz., we specified a topology with 14 interconnected CHAOS ECHO SER-VICEs, each simulating a different service in Sock Shop [9]. We also indicated the service mirroring Sock Shop's `edgeRouter` as a possible entry point for the application, listening on port 8080. The resulting application specification is publicly available at https://git.io/JnHTS). We then fed the CHAOS ECHO COMPOSER with such specification, obtaining a runnable Docker Compose file (also publicly available at https://git.io/JnHkq).

To actually run the experiment (and enable its repeatabiliy), we developed the script publicly available at https://git.io/JnHkP. The script iteratively deploys the obtained Docker Compose file by varying, at each iteration, the (a) services' failure rate, viz., P_FAIL, or (b) the number of their replicas. In each run of both (a) and (b), the services are configured to always invoke their backend services (viz., P_INVOKE is set to 100%). In each run of (b) services also have 0.5 probability of failing whilst processing an incoming request (viz., P_FAIL is set to 50%). Each run of both (a) and (b) deploys the application and exploits the CHAOS ECHO WORKLOAD GENERATOR to load its `edgeRouter` for 20 min, with requests spawned every 0.01 s. The script then processes the logs produced by each run to measure the average recovery time of services for such run, with such time measured as the interval between the service instance logging its "crash" and that of the service instance replacing the crashed one logging its readiness to accept incoming requests.

We run the script for five times on a Ubuntu 20.04 virtual machine featuring four vCPUs and 32 GB of RAM. The average recovery times measured in both considered scenarios are displayed in Fig. 4. We can observe that recovery times degrade in both considered scenarios, since the available computing resources get more and more loaded. In (a), this is because the Docker containers are "crashing" at a higher rate, bringing Docker Swarm to recover more and more containers. In (b), even if the failure rate is fixed, the more Docker containers are running, the less is the CPU time available for Docker Swarm to recover the "crashed" instances of the CHAOS ECHO SERVICEs. The orchestrator must indeed compete with higher numbers of running Docker containers, hence slowing recovery times. However, Fig. 4 clearly shows that the number of service replicas is by far more impacting on recovery time than failure rate.

The two scenarios in our experiment show how simple is to generate and configure testbed applications: this indeed just required writing a specification and a script for running the obtained testbed application under varying configurations. Doing the same with an existing application, like Sock Shop [9], would have instead required to intervene on its sources (or to integrate the application with some chaos testing tool) to ensure that —in each run of the experiment— some configurations remain fixed, e.g., backend services are always invoked, whilst some others vary in different run, e.g., service failure rates.

5   Conclusions

We have presented the CHAOS ECHO framework for automatically generating configurable cloud-native testbed applications. Given a specification of the topology of the desired application and the configuration of the CHAOS ECHO SERVICEs therein, the CHAOS ECHO COMPOSER automatically generates a deployable testbed application. Obtained testbed applications, triggered by the CHAOS ECHO WORKLOAD GENERATOR, can then be directly exploited to assess the performance of techniques devised for enforcing fault resilience in cloud-native applications, under varying running conditions of such applications. We showcased this in Sect. 4, where we shown the simplicity in setting up one such assessment with CHAOS ECHO.

We plan to further simplify the generation of testbed applications by enabling to visually edit them, e.g., in a web application displaying edited applications as in Fig. 1b. We also plan to enable further customising the behaviour of the CHAOS ECHO SERVICEs in a testbed application, by enabling to simulate e.g., different request processing times for different services, state-based behaviour, or different processings for error responses. We also plan to exploit testbed applications generated with CHAOS ECHO to assess existing techniques for enforcing fault resilience in cloud-native applications, e.g., to quantitatively compare the performance and accuracy of existing techniques for detecting failures and identifying their root causes [7].

References

1. Basiri, A., et al.: Chaos engineering. IEEE Softw. **33**(3), 35–41 (2016)
2. ChaosBlade.io: ChaosBlade. https://chaosblade.io
3. Kratzke, N., Quint, P.C.: Understanding cloud-native applications after 10 years of cloud computing - a systematic mapping study. J. Syst. Softw. **126**, 1–16 (2017)
4. Ledenev, A.: Pumba. https://github.com/alexei-led/pumba
5. Netflix: Chaos Monkey. https://netflix.github.io/chaosmonkey/
6. Pahl, C., Brogi, A., Soldani, J., Jamshidi, P.: Cloud container technologies: a state-of-the-art review. IEEE Trans. Cloud Comput. **7**(3), 677–692 (2019)
7. Soldani, J., Brogi, A.: Anomaly detection and failure root cause analysis in (micro)service-based cloud applications: a survey. CoRR abs/2105.12378 (2021)
8. Turnbull, J.: The Docker Book. Turnbull Press, New York (2014)
9. Weaveworks: Sock shop. https://microservices-demo.github.io
10. Zhou, X., et al.: Fault analysis and debugging of microservice systems: industrial survey, benchmark system, and empirical study. IEEE Trans. Softw. Eng. **47**(2), 243–260 (2021)

The Impact of Rare Container Restarts on Uninterrupted Kubernetes Operations

Szilárd Bozóki[1]([⊠]), Imre Kocsis[1], András Pataricza[1], Péter Suskovics[2], and Benedek Kovács[2]

[1] Department of Measurement and Information Systems, Budapest University of Technology and Economics, Magyar tudósok krt. 2, 1117 Budapest, Hungary
{bozoki,ikocsis,pataric}@mit.bme.hu
[2] Ericsson Hungary, Budapest, Hungary
{peter.suskovics,benedek.kovacs}@ericsson.com

Abstract. Container restart after failure is a key mechanism in the service availability management of containerized environments. However, container restart times empirically have long tail distributions, posing a risk for many soft real-time cyber-physical, telco and IoT systems, where service component downtimes have to remain under a specific threshold. We use Extreme Value Analysis (EVA) to model this long-tailedness. This paper provides an empirical demonstration of the influence of overall host resource utilization on long-tailedness. A solution to compare the impact of different container scheduling regimens on key metrics (as threshold-breaching restart times and availability) in edge-sized clouds is also presented. Application to our empirical results leads us to conclude that for edge deployments, threshold-breaching restart times are significantly sensitive to properly choosing container scheduling logic.

1 Introduction

Containerization has ushered in an era in which services can be practically realized through interdependent microservices deployed in a distributed manner. Compared to virtualization, the resource overhead of containerization is generally much lower and its operational management tasks usually complete much faster, making it increasingly a default choice in distributed application deployment from in-field devices to the data center. On top of the core technology, container orchestration solutions, such as Kubernetes, are responsible for automating deployment and managing applications.

Due to the basic characteristics of containerization, Kubernetes presides over a very dynamically reconfigurable environment. Consequently, it can be – and usually is – involved in the performance and dependability management of applications; e.g., by scaling out and in the number of container replicas based on their

---

This paper partially relies on a previous joint project between Ericsson and the Budapest University of Technology and Economics.

R. Adler et al. (Eds.): EDCC 2021 Workshops, CCIS 1462, pp. 109–119, 2021.
https://doi.org/10.1007/978-3-030-86507-8_11

resource utilization, providing platform level load-balancing between replicas or simply by automatically restarting crashed or stuck containers.

This way, in containerized deployments, meeting application service level agreements is an interplay between platform-level performance and dependability mechanisms, application-level ones and (although less and less) classic, human-in-the-loop operational management. However, how to appropriately co-design the platform and application level mechanisms to reach specific goals in extra-functional service characteristics is still ill-understood in general.

Our work tackles an important subset of this problem space: statistically characterizing container restart time as a function of overall host utilization. Earlier work has empirically shown that container restart times in typical Kubernetes environments have a long-tailed distribution [2].

For most general purpose, data center hosted applications this is not an issue. However, Kubernetes is increasingly used to manage edge cloud services, where application criticality meets relatively constrained resources (Typical critical edge applications will range from robotics, through autonomous vehicle control, to telemedicine). This means that on the one hand, the probability to meet constraints on maximum service outage times is a more important metric than availability; and on the other hand, "simple" container restarts probably will have to remain a blunt, but still important tool in the dependability toolbox.

In such a setting, the key design question is certainly *how can we characterize the ability to meet restart deadlines* and *how can we control it* – at least statistically? Our earlier observations indicated that the "long-tailedness" of container restart times on a host is influenced by host utilization – that is, the cumulative resource usage of the deployed containers (and other host processes, such as Kubernetes components). Consequently, appropriate deployment logic may be able to sufficiently constrain "long-tailedness" which is intolerably excessive from the application point of view. Starting from this hypothesis, our contributions in this paper are as follows:

- Using Extreme Value Analysis (EVA), to characterize container restart time distributions, we empirically show the impact of varying resource utilizations.
- We present a tool to calculate key single container as well as cluster-deployed container set portfolio metrics under hypothetical inputs – importantly, host set, deployment (in Kubernetes terminology: scheduler) logic and failure rate.
- By (representative) example, we use the tool to show that the choice of deployment logic can be key to constrain container restart time lengths.

2   Utilization Dependency of Restart Times

In a previous paper, we characterized restart time extremities of Kubernetes-managed containers using EVA [2]. In this section, we report on an experimental campaign where we collected data for increasing levels of CPU and IO background load and compare the EVA-provided extremity characteristics.

2.1 Experiments and Campaign

As infrastructure, our experiments used three identical Kubernetes clusters of *Dell PowerEdge R510* servers, with cluster id: 13, 52 and 67. The clusters were located in the same rack and connected through the same VLAN using a *Extreme Networks Summit X460-G2* switch.

As a measurement target, we intentionally selected one of the smallest publicly available container images, `BusyBox 1.3.1`, to minimise any size-related potential overheads. For each experiment, a test orchestrator application was deployed on a host in the cluster (without the co-deployment of other containers) and the target container was deployed on a different host in the same cluster (again, without the co-deployment of other containers).

For each experiment, the following scenario was performed:

– Setup: deployment of the target container (technically, a single-container *pod*) with a policy to automatically restart it on failure.
– Starting steady-state background load generation for $x\%$ CPU and $y\%$ IO utilization (both are experiment parameters).
– After a small holding time, `docker kill` is used for software implemented fault injection to simulate a container crash.
– The time between the `docker kill` and `docker start` life cycle events is measured as the *container restart time* (as no service runs in the container, in this case also the *container restoration time*) (Fig. 1).
– Cleanup of the target container.

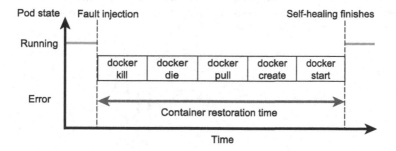

Fig. 1. Fault injection and components of the restart time

Based on preliminary measurements across the entire 0–100% ranges, the experimental campaign used 12 different (x, y) pairs: (0,0), (50,0), (80,0), (95,0), (0,5), (50,5), (80,5), (95,5), (0,40), (50,40), (80,40), (95,40). 1000 experiments were performed for each of these pairs.

For CPU background load generation, we used `stress-ng` with the `-c 0` parameter to load all cores and `-l 0..100` to specify load percentage. For IO load, we created a 10 GB file using the `dd` command, then copied it to the same directory using `rsync` and its `--bwlimit` parameter to control the IO load.

2.2   Exploratory Analysis

For visual exploratory analysis, we present the container restoration time observations for single resource background loads (Fig. 2) as well as those for dual
loads (Fig. 3) using bloxplots.

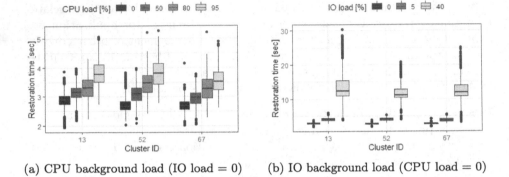

(a) CPU background load (IO load = 0)   (b) IO background load (CPU load = 0)

Fig. 2. CPU and IO load measurements

We observe that with no IO load, CPU load had a measurable ≈ linear impact
on container restart time. Also, with no CPU load, IO load had an impact which
was higher than the CPU load. Considering that the `busybox` container image
we used had a modest size of **1,22 MB**, a more complex application, with larger
IO (volumes) and image size needs, is likely to take even more time to restart.

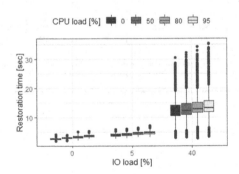

Fig. 3. CPU and IO dual loads for cluster 13

Observing the dual background load results, numerically there seems to be
an additive relationship between the mean/expected value of CPU and IO load
induced restoration time increases (as compared to the "undisturbed" case), as
expressed by Eq. 1 (X and Y stand for the different background loads):

$$E[X, Y] \approx E[X, 0] + E[0, Y] - E[0, 0] \tag{1}$$

From a practical point of view, if and when this empirical result holds (certainly not necessarily for all container types and environments – we are investigating the underlying mechanisms), single-resource experimental sweeps can support multi-resource restart time mean calculations. Note, however, that we can't state the same yet for the extremities (discussed in the next sub-section); the mathematics requires orders of magnitude larger numbers of observations than we have at the moment.

Also, as expected from identical hardware, the three clusters had almost the same results in restoration time average and variance. As a consequence, we will focus on the results of a single cluster (cluster 13) for the further analysis.

2.3   Characterizing Long-Tailedness

As discussed earlier, certain applications can't tolerate excessively long container restarts – which can happen even if the overall availability characteristics of a deployment are still acceptable with a wide margin. This is due to the simple fact that traditional statistics and probabilistic models usually suppress outlier (extreme) values, increasing the risk of seriously underestimating the frequency or the amplitude of the extreme events.

Characterizing container restart times is basically an exercise in *Measurement-Based Probabilistic Timing Analysis* (MBPTA): a discipline which uses probability theory and statistics on representative measured timing data, including *Worst-Case Execution Times* (WCET) [1,4,6]. The output of MBPTA is a probabilistic model: a fitted probabilistic WCET curve (pWCET). Faithfully capturing outliers in models – when they are important from the point of view of the application – is a significant challenge in MBPTA.

Extreme Value Analysis (EVA) is a mathematical tool explicitly targeting this problem and is becoming a dominant approach in MBPTA [3,5,8,9]. Informally, EVA approaches and the resulting models fall into one of two categories.

– *Annual Maxima Series* (AMS), a.k.a the *block maxima*, based on the Fisher – Tippett–Gnedenko theorem. AMS slices a dataset into equal "length" blocks (usually along time); selecting only the maximum value from each block.
– *Peak Over Threshold* (POT), a.k.a threshold exceedance, based on the Pickands – Balkema – de Haan theorem. POT selects all the values above a threshold, discards the rest, and uses *Generalized Pareto Distribution* (GPD) for the modelling of the selected values.

Both types of models are usually employed to answer risk-related as well as dimensioning queries. E.g., in hydrology, EVA models support computing *the probability of a given dam surviving the floods of the next time-period (e.g. 100 years)*, as well as the *height of a dam required to survive the floods of the next time-period with a given probability* – based on historical water height data.

Table 1 presents the data. The "POT" column contains the threshold used for selecting the values for GPD fitting in POT EVA. The "GOF" column contains the P-values of the statistical goodness of fit tests. Note that all the P-values are above 0.05, which means that there is no statistical evidence at this 0.05 significance level to reject the fitted GPD. The "DEP" column contains the calculated dependency (Eq. 1). See how "DEP" is close to the "Mean" column.

Table 1. Measurement data and metrics for cluster id 13

Configuration		Desc. stats		Extremity ind.			POT	GOF	DEP
CPU [%]	D.IO [%]	Mean [s]	Max [s]	Var.	Skew.	Kurt.	Thr. [s]	Pvalue	–
0	0	2.9	3.9	0.06	−0.52	4.68	3.08	0.93	–
0	5	4.0	5.9	0.34	0.27	2.96	5.38	0.64	–
0	40	13.6	30.4	17.94	1.22	4.53	20.80	0.93	–
50	0	3.1	4.0	0.07	−0.25	3.79	3.48	0.07	–
50	5	4.3	6.1	0.33	0.18	2.88	5.15	0.79	4.29
50	40	14.0	32.1	17.87	1.14	5.14	12.30	0.43	13.88
80	0	3.3	4.3	0.15	0.01	2.50	3.75	0.57	–
80	5	4.8	6.0	0.22	−0.15	2.81	5.18	0.93	4.47
80	40	14.2	34.2	17.29	1.27	6.10	15.55	0.21	14.06
95	0	3.9	5.1	0.18	0.29	2.80	4.10	0.64	–
95	5	5.1	6.8	0.33	0.11	2.81	5.55	0.93	4.97
95	40	15.0	35.4	19.35	1.45	6.77	18.90	0.29	14.57

3   Inferring KPIs from Container Restart Observations

To evaluate the impact of restart time on a "single application" and an "application portfolio" deployed on a Kubernetes cluster, we created a Java application (accompanied by R scripts) that supports:

- Running measurements on Kubernetes clusters (as described earlier) and estimating container restart time probabilistic WCET characteristics, using GPD to create cumulative distribution functions (CDFs).
- Creation of different container deployment regimens (intended to model different Kubernetes scheduler logics) and deriving KPIs at the "application portfolio" - a whole cluster or an edge site - level.

The two key components of WCET estimation and Deployment analysis are used to estimate container, node and (cluster) deployment KPIs as shown in Fig. 4. As input, a failure rate (more specifically, a Mean Time To Failure – MTTF – value) for the containers, container workload and the threshold where a restart event is considered "critically long" (i.e., threshold breaching) are required.

In this context, container workload is to be understood as the (currently CPU and IO) resource usage of a container. For the sake of simplicity, in this paper we assume constant workloads; this at most distorts our results by "erring on the safe side" (that is, we are creating pessimistic approximations by not taking into account the statistical multiplexing of varying resource usage profiles), as maximum resource usage can be enforced in Kubernetes on a per container basis.

Importantly, the container availability computed is *steady state* and we consider the restart-repair process to be independent from the failure (container crash) process. Also, we assume that the mean time to failure is significantly larger than the mean time to repair (MTTR; a realistic assumption for production IT systems). Under these constraints, the usual computation for availability applies [10] (Eq. 2).

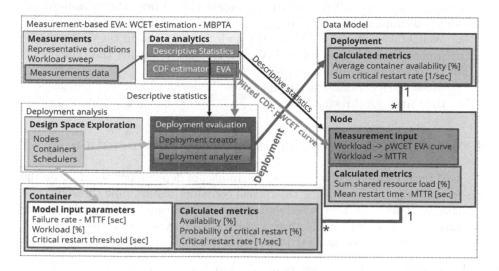

Fig. 4. Overview of method and data model

$$Availability = \lim_{t \to \infty} A(t) = \frac{MTTF}{MTTF + MTTR} \qquad (2)$$

For the sake of simplicity, the workloads and the critical restart time thresholds are simple scalars and not more sophisticated models (e.g., probability distributions for workloads). In future work, we plan to incorporate state of art workload modeling [7]. Multiple critical restart time thresholds – to represent severity classes as negligible, marginal, critical, and catastrophic (see IEC 61508) – are a straightforward extension of our current approach.

Container metrics are mostly self-explanatory, with *critical restart rate* being the average expected rate of critical restart occurrence. [1/sec]
Meanwhile, nodes have the following calculated metrics:

- **Sum shared resource load**: the sum workload deployed on the node. [%]
- **MTTR**: mean container restart time on the node with the workload [sec]

Deployments have the following calculated metrics:

- **Average container availability**: the average availability of containers. [%]
- **Sum critical restart rate**: the average rate at which critical container restarts are expected to occur in the deployment. [1/sec]

The derivation of calculated metrics is implemented through the following key stages and steps.

1. Process nodes:
   (a) Calculate the sum workload for each node
   (b) Get MTTR and EVA CDF for the sum workload from the measurements
2. Process containers by calculating
   (a) availability using MTTR from the node & MTTF form the container
   (b) probability of critical restarts (from EVA CDF & restart time threshold)
3. For the whole deployment, calculate
   (a) the average container availability
   (b) the sum critical restart rate

4   Deployment Design for Uninterrupted Operation

We used the presented tool to evaluate the impact of deployment decisions on the *cluster-wide* rate of not meeting the critical container restart time threshold and availability. Three different scheduling (container-placement) algorithms were implemented and considered in three variable-sweep experiment groups.
We implemented the following scheduler algorithms:

- **Round-robin (R)**: containers are deployed to the nodes of the cluster in the usual round-robin manner.
- **Greedy with availability target (A)**: containers are deployed sequentially, always to the host which results in a current partial deployment with the highest average container availability.
- **Greedy with criticality rate target (C)**: containers are deployed sequentially, always to the host which results in a current partial deployment with the lowest sum critical restart rate.

Currently, the greedy schedulers use brute force search in each step. All three schedulers adhere to node capacity constraints. The three experiment groups used all the schedulers and are described as follows:

Homogeneous container portfolio sweeps (HC): criticality threshold and container resource usages are fixed and homogenous; parameter sweep is performed on MTTF and node number. The number of containers was 10× the number of nodes in order to maintain a static overall resource utilisation. The aim of the sweep is to see how the schedulers compare in a laboratory environment with homogeneous containers.

Fixed container set and MTTF sweeps (100): MTTF, container number (100) and container resource usages are fixed. Sweep was performed on criticality threshold and number of nodes. All containers had the same criticality threshold. Essentially, this sweep aims at (1) testing the schedulers with changing overall resource utilisation, and (2) testing the effect of the criticality threshold.

Random portfolio with fixed 15 nodes sweeps (rand): The number of nodes is fixed, which represents a modest edge computing site. Essentially, this sweep aims at testing the schedulers in a real life like heterogeneous environment with fix resources. For each container, randomly (1) MTTF was selected from one of the six values: $1, 10, 100, \ldots 10^6$ s, (2) criticality threshold was selected between 0–30 s, (3) CPU load was selected from one of the four values: 9.5, 19, 28.5, 57%, (4) IO load was selected from one of the four values: 4, 8, 12, 24%. Regarding the number of containers, for a single deployment, new containers were created until the overall utilisation was over 76% CPU or 32% IO, or the number of containers reached 100. For a single deployment, if the random containers could not have been deployed to the 15 nodes owing to capacity constraints, then a new set of containers were randomly drawn. The process was iterated until 100 deployments were created.

Table 2. Design space exploration - parameter sweep map

Name	MTTF[s]	Sched.	#Nodes	#Cont.	Crit.t.[s]	CPU[%]	IO[%]
HC	$1, 10, 100, \ldots 10^6$	RAC	1,5,10,15	10,50,100,150	10	8	3
100	1000000	RAC	10,20,40,80	100	$2 \ldots 40$	8	3
rand.	rand.	RAC	15	rand.	rand.	rand.	rand.

Table 2 shows the parameter sweep groups. White denotes fixed properties, orange parameter-swept ones, cyan parameter-swept pairs, and red random values.

The merged utilisation in the figures is the average of CPU and IO utilisation.

4.1 Homogeneous Sweeps

The schedulers produced near identical results in the Homogeneous container portfolio case, which was expected from such pure homogeneous conditions.

Meanwhile, for the Fixed container set and MTTF sweeps, with also mostly homogeneous conditions, there was a difference between the schedulers. Moreover, we found a relation between resource utilisation vs critical restart rate and resource utilisiation vs availability (Fig. 5).

As expected, the criticality threshold had a large impact on the deployment criticality rate. Moreover, resource utilisation also had visible impact: as the workload increased, the penalty on criticality increased. The reasoning is that when adding a container to a node, all the containers on that node are affected.

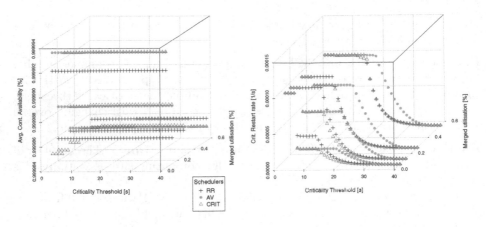

Fig. 5. Fixed container set and MTTF sweeps (100)

When optimizing for this kind of penalty, a good strategy is to optimize for an even workload throughout the entire deployment.

Generally speaking, for classic cloud settings with abundant host resources, large numbers of hosts and many tenants with largely uncorrelated workloads (which are piece-wise generally "small" compared to the hosts), the simple round-robin scheduler can be a good choice. However, edge clouds are expected to be limited in each of these aspects, therefore, the "proper packing" aspects of deployment gain heavy emphasis. Consequently, as we have shown, choosing a scheduler for the edge becomes an important design task.

4.2   Random Portfolio with Fixed 15 Nodes Sweeps

The random sweeps showed similar results, which reinforces our findings: there is room to optimize for criticality rate and availability with schedulers and extra resources (Fig. 6). As a rule of thumb for portfolio optimisation based on the results: the cluster wide average workload should be a KPI and the deviation from the cluster wide average workload should be penalised.

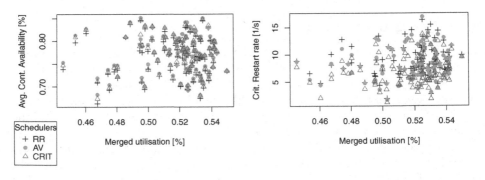

Fig. 6. Random portfolio with fixed 15 nodes sweeps (rand)

5 Conclusion

Restarting a container in Kubernetes is a basic resiliency mechanism. In critical applications, restart time has direct threshold requirements and also influences availability. In this paper, we demonstrated that container restart times can be long-tailed and are influenced by overall CPU and IO load on the host.

By numerically showing the impact of choosing a proper scheduler (deployment) logic on the cluster-level characteristics of container restart times, we have also demonstrated the importance of using restart time controlling (through workload distribution) schedulers for edge cloud settings.

References

1. Bernat, G., Colin, A., Petters, S.M.: Wcet analysis of probabilistic hard real-time systems. In: 23rd IEEE Real-Time Systems Symposium, 2002 (RTSS 2002). pp. 279–288 (2002)
2. Bozóki, S., et al.: Application of extreme value analysis for characterizing the execution time of resilience supporting mechanisms in Kubernetes. In: Bernardi, S., et al. (eds.) EDCC 2020. CCIS, vol. 1279, pp. 185–199. Springer, Cham (2020). https://doi.org/10.1007/978-3-030-58462-7_15
3. Castillo, E., Hadi, A., Balakrishnan, N., Sarabia, J.: Extreme Value and Related Models with Applications in Engineering and Science. Wiley, Hoboken (2004)
4. Cazorla, F.J., Kosmidis, L., Mezzetti, E., Hernandez, C., Abella, J., Vardanega, T.: Probabilistic worst-case timing analysis: taxonomy and comprehensive survey. ACM Comput. Surv. **52**(1) (2019). https://doi.org/10.1145/3301283
5. Cizek, P., Härdle, W.K., Weron, R. (eds.): Statistical Tools for Finance and Insurance, 2 edn. Springer, Heidelberg (2011). https://doi.org/10.1007/978-3-642-18062-0
6. Cucu-Grosjean, L., et al.: Measurement-based probabilistic timing analysis for multi-path programs. In: 2012 24th Euromicro Conference on Real-Time Systems. pp. 91–101 (2012)
7. Feitelson, D.G.: Workload Modeling for Computer Systems Performance Evaluation. Cambridge University Press, Cambridge (2015). https://doi.org/10.1017/CBO9781139939690
8. McNeil, A.J., Frey, R., Embrechts, P.: Quantitative Risk Management: Concepts. Princeton University Press (Techniques and Tools - Revised Edition), Princeton (2015)
9. Rakoncai, P.: On Modeling and prediction of multivariate extremes. Ph.D. thesis, Mathematical Statistics Centre for Mathematical Sciences, Lund University (2009)
10. Trivedi, K.S., Bobbio, A.: Reliability and Availability Engineering: Modeling, Analysis, and Applications. Cambridge University Press, Cambridge (2017)

EA Blueprint: An Architectural Pattern for Resilient Digital Twin of the Organization

Farid Edrisi[1]([✉]), Diego Perez-Palacin[1], Mauro Caporuscio[1],
Margrethe Hallberg[2], Anton Johannesson[3], Claudia Kopf[2],
and Johanna Sigvardsson[3]

[1] Linnaeus University, Växjö, Sweden
{farid.edrisi,diego.perez,mauro.caporuscio}@lnu.se
[2] Scania AB, Oskarshamn, Sweden
{grethe.hallberg,claudia.kopf}@scania.se
[3] Virtual Manufacturing AB, Göteborg, Sweden
{anton.johannesson,johanna.sigvardsson}@virtual.se

Abstract. Advancements in Cyber-Physical Systems, IoT, Data-driven methods, and networking prepare the adequate infrastructure for constructing new organizations, where everything is connected and interact with each other. A Digital Twin of the Organization (DTO) exploits these infrastructures to provide an accurate digital representation of the organization. Beyond the usual representation of devices, machines and physical assets supplied by Digital Twins, a DTO also include processes, services, people, roles, and all other relevant elements for the operation of organizations. Therefore, DTO can play a key role in realizing and analyzing aspects of organizations, assisting managers on the knowledge of the organization status, and foreseeing possible effects of potential changes in the organization. However, due to the dynamic, open, and ever-changing environment of organizations, an established DTO will soon degrade or even lose all its utility. Therefore, a DTO needs to evolve to recover its utility when the organization changes. The development of flexible, resilient, and easy to evolve DTO has not been well-addressed yet. Most of the existing proposals are context-dependent, system-specific, or focus on providing solutions in high-level abstraction. This work leverages Enterprise Architecture to propose an architectural pattern to serve as a blueprint toward the development of resilient DTO.

Keywords: Resilient Digital Twin of Organization · Enterprise architecture · Architectural pattern

1 Introduction

Organization's structures and processes are affected by changes in the environment, e.g., the market or regulations. Organizations need to adapt quickly

R. Adler et al. (Eds.): EDCC 2021 Workshops, CCIS 1462, pp. 120–131, 2021.
https://doi.org/10.1007/978-3-030-86507-8_12

to these forces, in order to be resilient and mitigate risks while taking advantage of opportunities they create: *forces drive the velocity of change*. A resilient organization should be therefore agile and responsive to changes, continuously adapting its capabilities, processes, strategies and information to meet changing objectives.

In the digitalization era, a Digital Twin of the Organization (DTO) plays a key role, as it allows for continuously simulating, analyzing, and monitoring the organization. DTO is defined as an accurate digital representation of the organization [20]. That is, DTO represents all the organizational elements (e.g., devices, processes, services, and people) as models that can be continuously simulated and analyzed in continuous assessment and optimization of the organization [14].

In order to fully benefit from DTO, the physical organization and developed DTO must be aligned. However, the continuous change of organizations creates misalignments between the physical organization and DTO, which reduces the DTO utility and acceptance within the organization.

In an ideal situation, evolutions in the physical organization and DTO would occur simultaneously and misalignments would not exist. However, in real situations, misalignments frequently happen. When the forces drive the change to actuate, neither physical organization can wait for the evolution of the DTO to execute its change, nor the evolution needed in the physical organization is completely well-defined in advance for the DTO developers. This creates the necessity of building *resilient DTO* which can cope with the disturbance in the alignment between DTO and physical organization caused by the changes in the organization.

Although the literature presents extensive discussions about the possible applications of DTO, there is still a lack of established engineering practices for architecting, developing, and operating flexible, resilient, and easy to evolve DTO. This prevents industry to fully benefit from DTO, as available solutions are either context-dependent or system-specific and challenging to adapt, maintain, and evolve.

There exist major open challenges in the construction of resilient DTO. We have previously discussed a set of architectural issues when developing a DTO [5], and have argued the need of defining an Architectural Framework that includes: (1) an *Architectural Pattern* achieving flexibility, (2) a *Reference Model* decomposing functionality into architectural elements, and (3) a *Reference Architecture* mapping the Reference Model onto physical elements. This work aims to address the first point by proposing an *Architectural Pattern* to facilitate the development of resilient DTO. According to the resilience classification in [3,4], it focuses on DTO resilience as *flexibility* (this property is also called flexibility in [16], and it is similar to the graceful extensibility and sustained adaptability properties in [21]).

To this end, we leverage *Enterprise Architecture* [17] (EA) to serve as a blueprint for developing the resilient DTO. In fact, EA is by default positioned to play a key role in realizing a DTO, as it embeds all the *principles* and *models* used in the realization of an organization: the *Business architecture* provides the structural and behavioral models, whereas the *Information Architecture* provides the data representing the actual status of the organization. The proposed architectural pattern, named EA Blueprint Pattern, fosters the use of (*i*) Service-Oriented Architecture (SOA) for instantiating the *Business Architecture*, and (*ii*) Model-View-Controller (MVC) for instantiating the *Information Architecture*. Further, the architectural pattern includes an additional element serving as a synchronization and alignment point in between digital models and real-time data coming from the real world.

The remainder of this paper has been organized as follows. Section 2 introduces the context of the resilient DTO and an example. Section 3 presents the proposed architectural pattern. Section 4 reports recent related works regarding Digital Twin architecture. Finally, Sect. 5 concludes the paper by addressing future research directions.

2   Resilient DTO Context

This works adopts the concept of system resilience defined in [7], which builds upon the concept of dependability, *the persistence of system dependability when facing changes*. We refer to types of changes in the organization using the terminology in the resilience framework in [4], which also conforms to the definition in [7].

The resilience framework in [4] distinguishes two kinds of changes that affect systems resilience, and two additional dimensions for the changes that are orthogonal to the two kinds of changes.

The two kinds of changes are called *operational changes* and *evolutionary changes*. Operational changes are changes that cause a modification of the system state. That is, the required DTO functionality remains the same, but its operational conditions are different. Evolutionary changes are changes that cause a modification of the acceptance criterion of the DTO; i.e., the DTO state can remain the same, but its expected functionality has evolved. The architectural pattern proposed in this work focuses on the DTO resilience when facing evolutionary changes.

The two orthogonal dimensions are the *readiness* of the system to cope with a change, and the *persistence* of the change in the system. Regarding the *readiness*, this work helps to deal with evolutionary changes that are *unexpected* or *expected-unhandled*; i.e., the current DTO is not equipped with mechanisms to handle them. Expected unhandled changes can happen when an organization explores a new business opportunity. Even if that is a planned event and the change is expected, there is high uncertainty how the organization will new develop and consolidate the new business branch and, thus, the DTO cannot be ready and aligned to the physical organization when the evolutionary change happens. In turn, examples of unexpected evolutionary changes in the organizations can be: forced quick changes in the organization business to endure new market trends and avoid going out of business, or the change in functionality of a public hospital when it must handle a surprising pandemic. Regarding the *persistence* of the change, this work focuses on *permanent* changes; i.e., the DTO will need to evolve because the evolutionary change will not disappear in a reasonable time horizon.

Since not all evolutionary changes cause the same level of damage or misalignment in the DTO, different DTO evolution tasks should be able to get different priority. An evolutionary change that causes a "minor" damage can still allow the DTO to provide some acceptable functionality even if not fully aligning with the physical organization. However, an evolutionary change in the physical organization can also cause a "major" damage in the DTO (e.g., restructuring the behavior or processes in the organization, adding new functionalities or business branches, or changing the format of input data streams). In that case, the DTO will soon degrade or even lose all its utility and functionality. Therefore, the DTO needs to evolve with high priority to regain its utility in the organization. Since several evolutionary changes can simultaneously coexist in the organization, it is necessary to build DTO whose parts can evolve independently. This allows prioritizing the evolution of the parts of the DTO that caused the greatest degradation in the DTO functionality.

It is worth noting that this work concentrates only on DTO that are resilient to evolutionary changes in the physical organization. The utilization of DTO for improving the organization's resilience is another very interesting and challenging research topic which it is out of the scope of this work.

2.1   Example of Resilient DTO

The utilization of Digital Twins has already been extensively reported for cases of devices, machinery and manufacturing processes in production plants. The proposed architectural pattern for DTO partially learns from experience in those domains, but the utilization of DTO is not restricted to organizations that are manufacturing plants or industry. To illustrate the DTO resilience challenges that exist in other types of organizations, the following paragraphs show an example where the organization is a public hospital.

The hospital consists of various departments or sections offering acute services, e.g. an emergency department, burn unit, surgery, and urgent care. It also includes more specialist units like cardiology or coronary care unit, intensive care unit, neurology, and obstetrics and gynecology, etc. Moreover, there are several roles of staff working in the hospital, such as doctors, nurses, janitors, administrators, etc. A DTO is already in place and represents all the hospital processes and elements aforementioned. It helps to dynamically optimize the hospital operations, scheduling, and utilization of resources. The DTO is also used by management to estimate the free resources in the near future in order to notify nearby hospitals about its capabilities to accept their patients in the next days, if necessary.

In 2020, the Covid-19 pandemic strikes hard. The hospital has to evolve its functionality quickly. Dedicating more staff, wings, beds and other types of equipment to Covid-19 patients, changing work shifts, canceling non-emergency surgeries, separating intensive care unit into sections to minimize infections, etc.

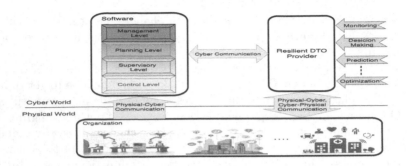

Fig. 1. DTO high-level view

are some of the required changes. In addition, tracking the patients' pathway and monitoring their situations frequently for taking necessary actions in major risks are other new tasks for the hospital managers. In this pandemic situation, a DTO would offer very useful functionality and support to the hospital new operations.

However, since there has been an unexpected evolutionary change in the organization, the current DTO is misaligned and, thus, it is almost useless in assisting the new activities that are critical for the hospital. The DTO must evolve. A resilient DTO would be able to evolve quickly.

3   The EA Blueprint Pattern

To help the development of resilient DTO, this section presents the EA Blueprint Pattern, an architectural pattern aiming at facilitating resilient DTO development and evolution.

Context: You are developing the resilient DTO Provider (see Fig. 1) mirroring the structure and behavior of a given organization by modeling and receiving the data of its physical and cyber elements to use in various applications. Since the organization is in continuous change and evolution, frequent misalignment could happen between DTO and real organization. So, DTO must be flexible and able to change and evolve accordingly.

Problem: How to develop a resilient DTO to evolve it according to the organization needs?

Forces:

- Resilient DTO elements should be developed according to Agile Design Principles [10] – i.e., Single responsibility, Open/closed, Liskov substitution, Dependency inversion, and Interface segregation –, so that they can be developed, deployed and evolved independently.
- Data should be shared with other software systems in the organization.

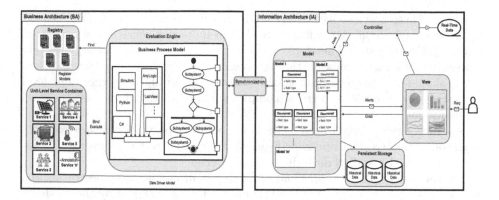

Fig. 2. The EA Blueprint Pattern

Solution: The EA Blueprint Pattern builds on EA concepts [17], and consists of three macro components (see Fig. 2): (1) *Business Architecture* (BA) represents business processes and interactions at organization level, (2) *Information Architecture* (IA) provides the technology infrastructure, the business application logic, and the data representing the current status of the organization, and (3) *Synchronization* handles the information exchange between BA and IA.

Resulting Context: Stable and flexible architecture, as new DTO elements can be easily added as services. Services are cohesive and loosely coupled.

Related Patterns: Service Oriented Architecture, Model View Controller.

3.1   Business Architecture (BA)

The *Business Architecture* is well positioned to play a key role in realizing a DTO, as it embeds *models* and *processes* that should be mimicked by the DTO. Since the organization is a dynamic entity continuously evolving in response to external forces (e.g., market trends, macro-economics) [2], its DTO should be easily evolved. To this end, EA Blueprint Pattern promotes the exploitation of Service-Oriented composition/decomposition style and Agile Design principles [10] to implement the BA. Indeed, such a combination improves DTO *modularity*, allows for different levels of *granularity*, and facilitates evolution [5].

In particular, the BA consists of three architectural elements: *Unit-Level Service Container*, *Registry*, and *Evaluation Engine* (see left-end side in Fig. 2).

The *Unit-Level Service Container* is in charge of managing the deployment and provision of organization services in DTO. Unit-Level Services serve as digital representations (models) of organizational elements – such as machines, spaces, activities, buildings, software and people – and provide their actual status and behavior. In Sect. 2.1, for the Hospital example, each unit that gives service is considered as a *Unit-Level Service*. For example, *Unit-Level Service Container* includes emergency unit, brain unit, surgery unit, cardiology or coronary care unit, etc. These services have some attributes like their capacity, IDs, certain equipment, and so on. According to SOA, the unit-level services are registered in the service *Registry*. Therefore, when elements in the physical organization change or are added/removed, their representation in *Unit-Level Service Container* should also be changed or added/removed accordingly. Further, unit-level services can be composed to create complex functionality and increase the level of abstraction.

As some services might need to perform complex analysis on *Historical Data* (e.g., computing trends or possible futures), they can directly access the *Persistent Storage* in IA and retrieve the data of interest.

On the other hand, the *Evaluation Engine* is in charge of orchestrating the unit-level services to implement the DTO behavior, as specified by the *Business Process Model*.

Since the organization is in continuous change, both the unit-level services and the business processes may need frequent evolution. Propagating the changes at the unit-level to allow the *Evaluation Engine* to always invoke the latest service version may overwhelm DTO maintainers. Moreover, not all changes in the organization are completely disruptive for the DTO. On the contrary, some parts of the Business Process Model can continue working acceptably well after an evolutionary change that modifies the DTO required functionalities. In these cases, even if the BA degrades its utility because it uses partially aligned versions of the unit-level services, it still provides some functionality to the organization.

For these reasons, the unit-level services are registered in the *Registry* including their version, so that *Evaluation Engine* can find and dynamically bind to the most appropriate version.

3.2 Information Architecture (IA)

The Information Architecture macro-component is in charge of: (*i*) handling the data streams from organization elements, collecting the raw data, and creating the information needed at the business level, (*ii*) handling the persistence of historical data, (*iii*) and visualizing the information of interest.

To this end, EA Blueprint Pattern leverages Model-View-Controller (MVC), as it is a suitable pattern for providing the aforementioned functionalities (see right-end side of Fig. 2). However, other patterns may also be considered as alternatives for implementing this macro component.

The *Controller* entity handles the real-time data streams from organizational elements (e.g., sensors, IoT devices, cameras, IT applications, etc.) embedded in the organization. Incoming data are either Time-based or Event-driven. Time-based data streams pass to the controller with a specific sample time. Event-driven data are received by occurring an event in the physical world while carrying important information about the event. The *Controller* processes data and feeds them into the *Model*. *Controller* is also responsible for manipulating the data according to the common representation defined by the *Model*.

Consequently, the controller is the first entity in providing resiliency regarding the Operational Changes. Data transmission problems are frequent when working with data streams from multitude of sources and IoT devices. For example, when a sensor is replaced by a new sensor sending data in a different format, the *Controller* needs to be updated to produce meaningful updates in the *Model*. In addition, hardware failures, connection loss, low battery, electromagnetic noise, or human errors providing inputs or disconnecting devices are potential problems lead to Operational or Evolution changes. Therefore, a combination of graceful degradability and recoverability may suffice for the *Controller*, but robustness to changes would also be optimal and achievable in some cases.

The *Model* represents the (real-time) information needed at the organization level. Indeed, the information retained by the *Model* depends on the semantics of the data streams, but is agnostic to the specific format. The *Model* is also responsible for sending the data to the *Persistent Storage*. Due to security issues, it is recommended that the *Model* establishes as few communications as possible with the persistent storage.

The *View* offers GUI for visualizing the organization status and other information of interest.

3.3 Synchronization

In order to fully transfer an organization into a DTO, a key requirement for the BA is to be *aligned* with the supporting IA. The *Synchronization* element in EA Blueprint Pattern is responsible for feeding BA with real-time information from the IA.

The *Synchronization* element is necessary to use the DTO beyond the evaluation (e.g. using data analytics, simulation, machine learning) of possible future scenarios using historical data. These evaluations focus on what could happen in the organization (what-if scenario), but not on what is currently happening [8]. However, constant change can quickly make the evaluation outdated and the manual task of re-configuring an evaluation technique to incorporate recent changes makes it cumbersome. Therefore, EA Blueprint Pattern includes a first-class element that deals with the synchronization of real-time information at business level.

Despite the apparent conceptual simplicity for this element, a recent study of methods concerning the connection of real-time data with their related models demonstrates that the majority of methods in this field are non-standard [11].

In EA Blueprint Pattern, the *Business Process Model* at the BA accepts external information through ports, which are designed to inject into the *Business Process Model* specific real-time data retrieved from the *Model*. In this regard, two important steps should be performed for synchronizing the data: (1) identifying the two specific points in the BA and IA that must be aligned, and (2) effectively and efficiently feeding the BA with real-time information. The first step could be done based on knowledge of the organization by identifying the digital IDs of different organizational elements. For the second step, the *Synchronization* entity converts the received data to interpretable format for models in *Evaluation Engine*. Then, depending on data types, time-based or event-driven, sends the received data to the associated device model recognized in the first step.

Synchronization entity is also the second main actor to handle *Operational Changes*. For doing this, it needs the support of a dependable Controller in the IA since it relies on the information created by the controller when the *Operational Change* happened. Since the BA needs meaningful information in order to perform its tasks, the synchronization component should take special care on synchronizing the BA with information that was recorded in the IA when a disturbance happen in a data stream.

4 Related Work

Literature related to this work is manifold and spans over different topics, from Software Architecture and Architectural Patterns to Digital Twin Architecture. While Software Architecture and Architectural Patterns have been extensively investigated [13], Digital Twin Architecture is a relatively new field. Therefore, we summarise hereafter the state-of-the-art in Digital Twin Architectures.

Josifovska et al. [6] propose a reference framework for developing Digital Twins of cyber-physical systems organized according to the five-level architecture. In particular, the Digital Twin framework is structured around four main building blocks including Physical Entity Platform, Virtual Entity Platform, Data Management Platform, and Service Platform.

Generic Digital Twin Architecture (GDTA) relies on 5D-Digital Twin Model [19] and align with the information technology layers of the Reference Architecture Model Industry 4.0. GDTA is composed of five layers including: Asset Layer—The physical, Integration Layer, Communication Layer, Information Layer, Functional Layer, and Business Layer. In particular, the Functional Layer represents the core of this architecture and consists of five different sections: Simulation Services, Monitoring Services, Diagnosis Services, Prediction Services, Control Services, and Reconfiguration Services.

Redelinghuys et al. [12] propose a six-layer architecture as a solution for a specific manufacturing case study. The architecture includes an IoT Gateway layer to transfer information between the physical and virtual space, a cloud-based data storage, and an emulation and simulation layer.

Talkhestani et al. [18] describe an architecture of a Digital Twin in an intelligent automation system. In particular, the proposed architecture consists of two parts: a Digital Twin, and an Intelligent Digital Twin. The Digital Twin architecture includes models and interfaces to related modeling tools, models' version management, operational, organizational and technical data, relations to other DTs and to the real world. Whereas, the Intelligent Digital Twin is one level higher and enables for optimization of the process flow, automatic control code generation for newly added machines, and predictive maintenance.

Malakuti et al. [9] identify, as a result of interviews with different experts and reviews of existing proposals, nine requirements that should be fulfilled by Digital Twins. In order to fulfill such requirements, they introduce an abstract layered architecture for building digital twins and synthesizing the information from different sources.

Alam et al. [1] propose a digital twin architecture reference model for cloud-based cyber-physical systems (C2PS). The suggested architecture includes five layers. First and second layers have been allocated to physical and cyber entities, respectively, where every physical entity is straightforwardly mapped to a digital representative hosted in the cloud. A one-to-one connection between digital and physical entities is assumed for synchronizing the state of physical objects and their digital representative in the cloud. The third layer is responsible for communication and networking, whereas the fourth layer acts as a middleware managing digital entities, their active relations, and the related ontologies. Finally, the last layer is in charge of managing the visibility and privacy of the entities as well as of handling the data consumption and visualization from stakeholders.

All the aforementioned works provide general solutions, at different level of abstractions, pointing out the need for having an architectural entity (e.g., layer, component) specifically dedicated to DTO. However, none of them detail how to develop such a specific entity. Also, discussing on the need for resilient DTO is the missing part of these works. On the other hand, several papers leverage DTO to reach an organization or system resiliency like [15] which is not in the scope of this paper.

5   Conclusion

A Resilient Digital Twin of the Organization (DTO) is capable to keep or recover its utility and functionality in confronting different types of organizational changes. Although developing a Resilient DTO is a grand challenge, it facilitates actualizing of a resilient organization. Therefore, the current paper has investigated how to develop a resilient DTO to evolve according to the organization's needs. As the result, EA Blueprint Pattern has been proposed. This pattern, leveraging Enterprise Architecture, offers an architectural pattern that consists of three Macro components: (*i*) Business Architecture (BA), (*ii*) Information Architecture (IA), and (*iii*) Synchronization element. BA mimics the business processes and interactions at organization level whereas IA is responsible for managing real-time data. Synchronization handles the information exchange between BA and IA.

Acknowledgements. This research is funded by the Swedish Knowledge Foundation, Grant No. 20200117: ALADINO – ALigning Architectures for DIgital twiN of the Organization.

References

1. Alam, K.M., El Saddik, A.: C2PS: a digital twin architecture reference model for the cloud-based cyber-physical systems. IEEE Access **5**, 2050–2062 (2017)
2. Andersson, J., Caporuscio, M.: Aligning architectures for sustainability. In: Proceedings of the 10th European Conference on Software Architecture Workshops, ECSAW 2016 (2016)
3. Andersson, J., Grassi, V., Mirandola, R., Perez-Palacin, D.: A distilled characterization of resilience and its embraced properties based on state-spaces. In: Calinescu, R., Di Giandomenico, F. (eds.) SERENE 2019. LNCS, vol. 11732, pp. 11–25. Springer, Cham (2019). https://doi.org/10.1007/978-3-030-30856-8_2
4. Andersson, J., Grassi, V., Mirandola, R., Perez-Palacin, D.: A conceptual framework for resilience: fundamental definitions, strategies and metrics. Computing **103**(4), 559–588 (2020). https://doi.org/10.1007/s00607-020-00874-x
5. Caporuscio, M., Edrisi, F., Hallberg, M., Johannesson, A., Kopf, C., Perez-Palacin, D.: Architectural concerns for digital twin of the organization. In: Jansen, A., Malavolta, I., Muccini, H., Ozkaya, I., Zimmermann, O. (eds.) ECSA 2020. LNCS, vol. 12292, pp. 265–280. Springer, Cham (2020). https://doi.org/10.1007/978-3-030-58923-3_18
6. Josifovska, K., Yigitbas, E., Engels, G.: Reference framework for digital twins within cyber-physical systems. In: 2019 IEEE/ACM 5th International Workshop on Software Engineering for Smart Cyber-Physical Systems, pp. 25–31 (2019)
7. Laprie, J.C.: From dependability to resilience. In: DSN 2008 (2008)
8. Lu, Y., Liu, C., Wang, K.I.K., Huang, H., Xu, X.: Digital twin-driven smart manufacturing: connotation, reference model, applications and research issues. Robot. Comput.-Integr. Manuf. **61**, 101837 (2020)
9. Malakuti, S., Schmitt, J., Platenius-Mohr, M., Grüner, S., Gitzel, R., Bihani, P.: A four-layer architecture pattern for constructing and managing digital twins. In: Bures, T., Duchien, L., Inverardi, P. (eds.) ECSA 2019. LNCS, vol. 11681, pp. 231–246. Springer, Cham (2019). https://doi.org/10.1007/978-3-030-29983-5_16
10. Martin, R.C.: Agile Software Development: Principles, Patterns, and Practices. Prentice Hall PTR, Hoboken (2003)
11. Modonia, G.E., Caldarolaa, E.G., Saccob, M., Terkajb, W.: Synchronizing physical and digital factory: benefits and technical challenges. Procedia CIRP **79**, 472–477 (2019)
12. Redelinghuys, A.J.H., Basson, A.H., Kruger, K.: A six-layer architecture for the digital twin: a manufacturing case study implementation. J. Intell. Manuf. **31**(6), 1383–1402 (2019). https://doi.org/10.1007/s10845-019-01516-6
13. Richards, M.: Software Architecture Patterns. O'Reilly Media Inc., Sebastopol (2015)
14. Rosen, R., von Wichert, G., Lo, G., Bettenhausen, K.D.: About the importance of autonomy and digital twins for the future of manufacturing. IFAC-PapersOnLine **48**(3), 567–572 (2015). 15th IFAC Symposium on Information Control Problems in Manufacturing
15. Saad, A., Faddel, S., Youssef, T., Mohammed, O.A.: On the implementation of IoT-based digital twin for networked microgrids resiliency against cyber attacks. IEEE Trans. Smart Grid **11**(6), 5138–5150 (2020)
16. Schmeck, H., Müller-Schloer, C., Çakar, E., Mnif, M., Richter, U.: Adaptivity and self-organization in organic computing systems. ACM Trans. Auton. Adapt. Syst. **5**(3), 10:1–10:32 (2010)

17. Sousa, P., Caetano, A., Vasconcelos, A., Pereira, C., Tribolet, J.: Enterprise architecture modeling with the unified modeling language. In: Rittgen, P. (ed.) Enterprise Modeling and Computing with UML, pp. 67–94. IGI Global (2007)
18. Talkhestani, B.A., et al.: An architecture of an intelligent digital twin in a cyber-physical production system. at - Automatisierungstechnik **67**(9), 762–782 (2019)
19. Tao, F., Zhang, M., Nee, A.: Five-dimension digital twin modeling and its key technologies. In: Digital Twin Driven Smart Manufacturing, pp. 63–81. Academic Press (2019)
20. Watts, S.: Digital twins and the digital twin of an organization (DTO). https://www.bmc.com/blogs/digital-twins
21. Woods, D.D.: Four concepts for resilience and the implications for the future of resilience engineering. Reliab. Eng. Syst. Saf. **141**, 5–9 (2015)

Assisting Developers in Preventing Permissions Related Security Issues in Android Applications

Mohammed El Amin Tebib[1]([⊠]), Pascal André[2], Oum-El-Kheir Aktouf[1], and Mariem Graa[3]

[1] Univ. Grenoble Alpes, Grenoble INP, LCIS, Valence, France
{mohammed-el-amin.tebib,oum-el-kheir.aktouf}@lcis.grenoble-inp.fr
[2] LS2N CNRS UMR 6004 - University of Nantes, Nantes, France
pascal.andre@ls2n.fr
[3] IMT ATLANTIQUE, Nantes, France
mariem.graa@telecom-bretagne.eu

Abstract. Permissions related attacks are a widespread security issue in Android environment. Permissions misuse enables attackers to steal the application rights and perform malicious actions. While most of the existing solutions are advocated from end-users perspective, we take in this paper the developers perspective because security should be a software design concern. We propose a formal specification covering the permissions use by the current developers of Android applications, who are almost a third party developers. We underline a set of security properties. Then, we formally verify them by applying a Model Driven Reverse Engineering approach that enables abstraction and property verification. We implement the analysis approach as an IDE plug-in called **PermDroid**. Finally, we show the applicability of our approach through a case study.

Keywords: Android · Development · Security · Privacy · Permissions · IDE · MDRE

1 Introduction

Smartphones with Android platform are the most used ones with a market share of 72.6% (May 2020)[1]. According to CVE details[2], the official MITRE datasource for Android vulnerabilities, 2020 and the beginning of 2021 have witnessed the most significant increase of Android security threats, which could lead to several security attacks such as: collusion, privilege escalation, and ransomware attacks. While most of existing solutions are advocated from the end-user perspective,

---

[1] https://gs.statcounter.com/os-market-share/mobile/worldwide/#monthly-201905-202005.

[2] https://www.cvedetails.com/product/19997/Google-Android.html?vendor_id=1224.

© Springer Nature Switzerland AG 2021
R. Adler et al. (Eds.): EDCC 2021 Workshops, CCIS 1462, pp. 132–143, 2021.
https://doi.org/10.1007/978-3-030-86507-8_13

like anti-malwares [3], system configurations [12, 20] and user-friendly tools [23], these security flaws are almost introduced at the development stage [13]. Developers often do not prioritize security during mobile applications development for various intrinsic and extrinsic reasons such as: (1) *lack of security skills*; (2) *scope of work*: developers leave this issue to security specialists, (3) *hardness*: security is a wide and difficult domain that slows down delivering the product in time. Despite real investment, security policies are therefore manually encoded into the application, which is a dangerous practice that may cause security breaches [2].

Among the security issues at development stage, we focus in this paper on permission related ones. Indeed, permissions are a main security concept to ensure the privacy protection, and restrict the access of third party libraries to the system resources. A recent experimentation study [19] realized on 574 GitHub repositories of open-source Android apps, showed that permissions-related issues are still a frequent phenomenon in Android apps. Android provides an official documentation to explain how to properly use permissions[3]. However, due to the continuous changes of permissions number and specification, this documentation becomes hardly readable for developers, leading to different security issues and drawbacks [11] such as: (i) Wrong permission usage: due to some permissions similarities, developers may intentionally use wrong permissions, *e.g.*: the use of *ACCESS_COARSE_LOCATION* instead of *ACCESS_FINE_LOCATION* (ii) Permissions over-privilege: a widespread phenomenon that occurs when the application declares more permissions than those actually used. The unused permissions can be exploited by hackers to perform malicious actions, especially ransomwares, (iii) Permissions under-privilege: occur when the application requires more permissions than those declared, which does not conform with the transparency principle that each developer should respect, (iv) Unprotected API: occurs when developers forget to add an exception handler to some API methods, which may throw exceptions.

In this paper we investigate the respect of permission security guidelines by the current developers of Android applications. We develop a formal framework for analyzing permission security issues like permissions naming conflicts, unauthorized access during component invocation, privilege escalation and permission over-privilege. The main contributions of this paper are: 1) A model based formal verification approach to assist third party developers in preventing the undesired permissions related behaviours that compromise the privacy of the application. 2) An implementation of the proposed approach in the form of an extensible IDE based tool (Eclipse, intellIJ, AndroidStudion) called **PermDroid** that identifies and prevents permission security risks and vulnerabilities related to the Android permission system. This tool analyzes up to the last Android API version 30. The rest of the paper is organized as follows. Section 2 presents the major permission security evolutions in Android versions. Section 3 describes the security mechanisms of Android with a special focus on permissions. We specify a set of security properties and guidelines in Sect. 4. The Analysis of these properties through an MDRE approach is presented in Sect. 5 and the experiments on a

---

[3] http://developer.android.com/sdk/api_diff/30/changes.

case study are provided in Sect. 6. Section 7 considers related works and finally, Sect. 8 concludes with a summary of our contributions and provides tracks for future work.

2 Android Permission System Evolution

The reader will find an interesting introduction to the Android Permission Model in [4]. In this section we quickly overview the most significant evolutions related to the Android permission system[4]. Table 1 summarizes the permissions-related security features categorized per Android version.

Table 1. Evolution of Android permission system

Ver. num	Version name	Security features
4	Kit kat	Permission groups
6	Marshmallow	Runtime permissions
8	Oreo	New access control mechanism
10	Ice cream sandwich	Permissions updates
11	Android 11	Permissions auto revoke

Since the creation of the first version of Android on 2008, its permission system has been under many studies related to Android security and privacy. The concept of *Permission* is introduced in the 4th version of Android "Kit Kat". Each application cannot access a sensitive information (*e.g.* contacts, SMS, location...) without having the required permissions. Those permissions could only be granted by the user at the installation time. Later in version 4, permissions groups were introduced to add a logical grouping of permissions sharing the same characteristics. If one of the permissions belonging to the same group is granted, the other permissions are automatically granted. The most significant update occurred on 2016. The user could avoid granting all permissions at install time. Indeed, the version (v6, API 23) brought large changes to the permission model enabling to partially check and grant permissions. Permission of normal category could be granted at install time and those of dangerous category could be checked and activated at run-time only; permission can be revoked later [1]. Last but not least, in the version 10, Android provides a modular permission controller that enables to update privacy policies and UI elements (*e.g.* policies and UI related to granting and managing permissions). Android 11 recently added the support of auto revoke apps, where the new Permissions Controller module can automatically revoke runtime permissions for Apps that haven't been used for an extended period of time. Apps targeting SDK 30 or higher have

---

[4] https://www.techrepublic.com/article/ios-and-android-security-a-timeline-of-the-highlights-and-the-lowlights/.

auto revoke enabled by default, while apps targeting SDK 29 or lower have auto revoke disabled by default[5].

Many evolutions made Android a more secured environment. Without understanding these evolutions, it is getting harder for developers to design secured Android application with respect to the permission security guidelines. A deep and continuous analysis, documentation and understanding are required by different stakeholders, especially developers.

3   Permission Security Model

Using the expressive Z notation [21], we formalize the permissions concepts in Android application. Formalization enables to understand the essence of the permission system. Besides, it enables to state security properties we ought to verify in Sect. 4 and check on Android apps in Sect. 5. Due to space limitation, a detailed specification is provided in a web appendix[6].

We consider Android applications made of *Components* that communicate via *Intents*. Basically, components are categorized into two families: 1) foreground components such as activities and 2) background components such as Services, Broadcast Receivers, and Content Providers. Applications are made of components (*cApp*), which can be part of several applications, and intents (*iApp*). Components can be source or target of intents (*csrcInt, ctargInt*).

In Android applications (defined by the Z schema AndroidApps (See Footnote 6), *Permissions* are declared in the manifest.xml configuration file, and required at different stages: (1) system APIs interactions, (2) database access, (3) message passing system via intents, (4) invocation of specific protected methods in public APIs and (5) content provider data access. They also have different protection levels. The Z basic types assume the existence of an abstract set of permissions and the free type provides the permission categories.

[*PERMISSION*]
Category ::= *normal* | *dang* | *sig* | *sos*

Permissions are declared per application (*permApp*), components (*perm Comp*) and intents (*permIntent*). Component permissions are declared by components (*cpermDec*) and required by active components (*cpermReq*). Passive components provide read and write access permissions (*rpermDec, wpermDec*).

---

[5] https://source.android.com/devices/architecture/modular-system/permissioncontr oller.

[6] https://pagesperso.ls2n.fr/~andre-p/download/androidPerm.pdf.

AndroidPerm
AndroidApps
Permissions : $\mathbb{P}$ *PERMISSION*
decPermLevel : *PERMISSION* $\nrightarrow$ *Category*
permLevel : *PERMISSION* $\rightarrow$ *Category*
permApp : *Applications* $\leftrightarrow$ *Permissions*
permComp : *Components* $\leftrightarrow$ *Permissions*
permIntent : *Intents* $\leftrightarrow$ *Permissions*
cpermDec : *Components* $\leftrightarrow$ *Permissions*
cpermReq : *CompAct* $\leftrightarrow$ *Permissions*
rpermDec, wpermDec : *CompPas* $\leftrightarrow$ *Permissions*

---
dom *decPermLevel* $\subseteq$ *Permissions* $\wedge$
permLevel = (*Permission* $\rightarrow$ {*normal*}) $\oplus$ *decPermLevel*

ran *permApp* $\cup$ ran *permComp* = *Permissions* $\wedge$ ran *permIntent* $\subseteq$ *Permissions*

permComp = *cpermDec* $\cup$ *cpermReq*

(*rpermDec* $\cup$ *wpermDec*) = (*CompPas* $\lhd$ *cpermDec*)

Each permission belongs to one *Category* by *permLevel* ($\rightarrow$ is a total function). This category can be explicitly defined by *decPermLevel* (it is optional since $\nrightarrow$ is a partial function) and only the considered permissions have one dom *permLevel* $\subseteq$ *Permissions*. If no category is explicitly given, the level is *normal* ((*Permission* $\rightarrow$ {*normal*})$\oplus$*decPermLevel*). All considered *Permissions* are associated to applications or components by (*permApp* $\cup$ ran *permComp* = *Permissions*). Intents permissions are related to them by *permIntent* $\subseteq$ *Permissions*. Component permissions are declared or required (*permComp* = *cpermDec* $\cup$ *cpermReq*) but only active components require permissions. Passive components provide read and write access permissions (*rpermDec, wpermDec*) of the declared permissions of passive components ((*rpermDec* $\cup$ *wpermDec*) = (*CompPas* $\lhd$ *cpermDec*)). In the next section we formally specify security properties using the above formal descriptions.

4   PermDroid Security Properties

Referring to standards such as CIA (Confidentiality, Integrity, Availability) or AAA (Authorization, Authentication, Accounting) [9], we target confidentiality and authorization properties. Again for sake of space, only two properties are used in this paper but others are given in the web appendix (See Footnote 6). We refer here to [16] that investigated the mistakes committed by developers.

Component Invocation. As a component could perform sensitive actions, it should be protected against unauthorized accesses. *(p1) Two interacting components must have compatible permissions. Every required permission of a called component must be fulfilled by the caller component.*

_P1_ _____

| *AndroidPerm*
| *ca, cp* : *COMPONENT*
|_____
| $(ca, cp) \in interactions \Rightarrow cpermReq(\!|\ \{co\}\ |\!) \subseteq cpermDec(\!|\ \{ca\}\ |\!)$

Unprotected Components - Privilege Escalation. Exported components can be accessed by other applications including malicious apps. Referring again [16], a significant number of non protected exported components was found in on-line Android open source projects (19039 components overall 8749 application).

(P2) An exported component must declare permissions to be protected.

_P2_ _____

| *AndroidPerm*
|_____
| $cpermDec(\!|\ expComp\ |\!) \neq \emptyset$

Many related research studies [6,7,12] explore the dynamic behaviour of interacting applications to find permission related security flaws. Based on static analysis, we could only (1) determine the requested permissions declared in the manifest configuration file, (2) generate permissions used by the application through inspecting the permission related APIs, (3) inspect methods involving sending and receiving intents, (4) and methods involving the management of content providers. Whereas dynamic analysis could assist in (1) handling the dynamic loading of classes from embedded jar or apk files, (2) handling Java reflection (used by more than 57% of Android apps [15]).

Z/EVES System [17] enables not only syntax and type checking verification, but also the proof of operation assertions (pre/post conditions vs the state schema invariants) and theorems. The effective verifications are not provided here but the formalisation is an input for the implementation, where the rules will be written in OCL which is inspired from Z.

5 PermDroid Design and Implementation

In Sect. 4 we formalized five specific security related permissions issues coming from: permissions naming violations, unprotected components, components invocation, over-privileged permission use, and unprotected implicit intents. To assist developers (especially third party ones) to automatically prevent these issues in their implementations, we propose in this section a model-based approach using a security meta-model inspired from the formal model presented in Sect. 3 with some additional technical aspects[7]. The proposed approach is given in Fig. 1. It is based on three main steps (see Fig. 1): (1) Reverse engineering, (2) Model to Model (M2M) transformations, and (3) Analysis phase.

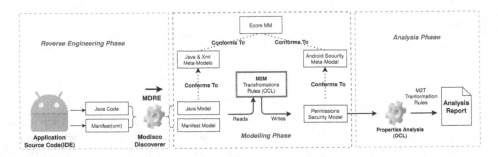

Fig. 1. PermDroid architecture

Reverse Engineering Phase (Model Discovery). Reverse engineering provides abstract models that capture the pertinent information for reasoning purposes. We used MoDisco[8] tool to perform the reverse engineering process. Basically, MoDisco provides a graphical representation of the program Abstract Syntax Tree AST[9] which makes the corresponding models it generates correct and perfectly conform to the source code. In addition, MoDisco supports this process for Java and XML based applications, which is relevant to study Android applications. We developed a set of Java scripts that take as input the manifest and the Java source files of an Android application, and generate as output the xmi corresponding model.

Model Transformation Phase. At the end of the first step, we apply a M2M transformation process using ATL[10] tool which is based on the OCL formal language. As a result of the model transformation process, we obtain the Android security model used for the analysis phase. A schematic view showing the whole model-driven chain is presented in phase 2 of Fig. 1.

The transformation engine we implemented is composed from a set of rules. Each one serves to *read* a specific part from the source model "Java or manifest models" and *write* the corresponding element in the target model following a well defined semantic. The following small OCL code shows the main rule of the transformation script that aims to generate an instance of *application* element

---

[7] See the web appendix (See Footnote 6).

[8] https://wiki.eclipse.org/MoDisco.

[9] https://www.vogella.com/tutorials/EclipseJDT/article.html.

[10] https://www.eclipse.org/atl/.

structure presented in the meta-model of Fig. 1 from the *root* XML element of the manifest file.

```
—@nsURI MM=www. eclipse . org/MoDisco/Xml/0.1. incubation/XML
—@path MM1=/safetyProperties/metamodels/androidapp. ecore
rule mainRule {
  from    manifest : MM! Root (manifest.name="manifest")
  to      securityModel : MM1! Application (
            name <- manifest.name,
            permissions <- MM1! Permission. allInstances (),
            components   <- MM1! Component. allInstances ())}
```

Security Properties Analysis Phase. For the analysis phase, we implemented using ATL a set of rules called *helpers* (like methods in Java but with a formal constraint format) to implement the security properties we specified in Sect. 4. To make clear the idea of how to use OCL for the analysis phase, we present in the following a simple part of the implemented helpers, but we do not put the whole rules due to space limitation.

```
helper def: permission_name_conflict (): Boolean =
   if ((thisModule.normalPermissions -> intersection (thisModule.
        dangerousPermissions))-> isEmpty ())
   then true      else false      endif;
```

The permission_name_conflict() is an example of helper that is used to implement permission property (P1). It parses the instance security model representing the Android application under analysis, to inspect if there is such permission with normal protection level that is also declared for a second time as dangerous permission. If the helper return type is true, our tool will notify the developer. We give an example on the use of PermDroid at the end of Sect. 6.

6 Experimentation

To experiment the ongoing work on PermDroid tool, we select a simple open source application called **Telegram** extracted from F_Droid[11], a famous repository for Android open source applications. It represents a messaging app with a main focus on speed and security. We add some modifications to the application in order to inject the security flaws we want to raise at the analysis phase. The goal is to validate the followed steps based on a simple case study.

Reverse Engineering (RE) Phase. As mentioned before, in the RE phase PermDroid will have as input the Android application code files (manifest.xml and Java classes). MoDisco provides an abstract representation of the manifest file. It exposes the *root* instance that represents the composite element by which we can access children items such us: components, intents, permissions and their attributes. For sake of space, we add on a the web appendix a detailed screenshot

---

[11] https://f-droid.org/app/org.telegram.messenger.

that presents the generated model representing the manifest configuration file of *Telegram* application.

Modelling Phase. Once the corresponding *Telegram* demo app models are generated, PermDroid launches the transformation process to generate the application security model displayed in Fig. 7 of web appendix, where types specified on our security meta-model are presented on the left side, and the existing instances for each type are presented on the right side. Based on these representation, we notice that the demo app is composed only from background components: 15 services, 18 broadcast receivers and 3 content providers.

Analysis Results. The final step is to launch the analysis of the security properties. Figure 2 shows the analysis results raised by PermDroid tool. The analysis report raises the unsatisfaction of the security property related to naming conflicts. It indicates that $perm1 = $ "BIND_TELECOM_CONNECTION_SERVICE" with $Nrml\_perm$ is duplicated in: "Content Provider":"notification_image_provider" with "Dangerous" protection level.

Fig. 2. Analysis results of *Telegram* demo app

7   Related Works

During the last decade, many research works exploring security gaps in Android permission system have been published. These works can be classified into two main classes.

System Analysis and reconfiguration approaches that mainly consider the weaknesses that reside on the system on one side, and the user knowledge limitations with regards to Android permission granting on the other side. The goal is to make the system environment safer by putting the malware applications apart from the system. In [14] a formal model of the Android permission framework using high level Petri nets is presented. It defines the complex relationships among different levels of permissions such as overall application-level permissions and component level permissions. In the same line, many other works are based on formal models and analysis [8,12] to verify the security mechanisms of Android. These works generally differ on the analysed Android version: [12] before version 6 where the permission granting occurs always at install time, and [8] after version 6 where permissions could be granted dynamically at runtime.

Other solutions basically require modification of the Android framework or apps' implementation logic. As an example we can cite [20] and [18] which change the permission management mechanism, and propose a new Android security model and isolation strategy respectively. These modifications will impose to a developer to change the usual way of manipulating the manifest configuration file, which makes this solutions too hard to be adopted by developers. *As we can see, most of the research related solutions are proposed from end users perspective. We conduct our research from a different design methodology. We tackle developers perspective because detecting permission security issues in an early stage will evade unnecessary vulnerabilities, and prevent the potential for abuse by SDKs.*

Developer's perspective approaches aim to automate the assistance to developers who are almost not aware about security issues introduced during the development stage. There are few related works aiming to assist developers identifying permission related security issues. A big parts of these works focuses on over-privilege permissions issue; they propose integrated IDE solutions to help developers make better decision about the permission use. The goal is to help the developer in building apps with the least required permissions, like works in [5,10,22] that statically analyse the manifest and the Java code, and separate between two sets of permissions: (1) the declared permissions set and (2) the used permission set. The idea is that to reach least privilege principle, the application should not declare more permissions than those used. In the same line [24] gives a more accurate analysis and adds analysis capacities to cover underprivileged permissions and unprotected APIs in addition to over-privileged ones. The main limitations of these tools are that the used permission-function pairs are generated for only specific Android API levels (2.2 for [22] and 5 for [5]). Furthermore, all of them are static analysis tools, while the big part of used permissions will be granted during run-time. This limitation will reduce the accuracy of *used permission* set content.

Our approach belongs to this class of solutions. We benefit from formal methods to perform high level analysis for developers. We follow a similar methodology as done by [24], where they benefit from system analysis studies like [3] to provide to developers an automatic solution helping them detecting if their code does not respect the least privilege principle.

8   Conclusion and Future Work

This work constitutes a basis for the development of a well-defined formal framework called PermDroid that assists developers in preventing permission security related-issues. The starting point was to define a formal specification that covers the minimum number of concepts related to permissions used in the context of a single application. This formalization helped us to define some security properties that are verified using an automated approach based on MDRE. We finally experimented the implemented architecture through a simple case study.

Ongoing and future works consider the extension of studied security properties, and the integration of dynamic analysis to our approach. This will contribute to handle dynamic loading of classes and Java reflection. The expected final outcome of our work is a flexible integrated tool that implements our approach and can be integrated in several IDEs. Finally, we aim to experiment our approach on a large data set, and evaluate its usability through organizing controlled practical dev sessions.

References

1. Almomani, I.M., Khayer, A.A.: A comprehensive analysis of the Android permissions system. IEEE Access **8**, 216671–216688 (2020). https://doi.org/10.1109/ACCESS.2020.3041432
2. Armando, A., Carbone, R., Costa, G., Merlo, A.: Android permissions unleashed. In: 2015 IEEE 28th Computer Security Foundations Symposium, pp. 320–333. IEEE (2015)
3. Au, K.W.Y., Zhou, Y.F., Huang, Z., Lie, D.: PScout: analyzing the android permission specification. In: Proceedings of the 2012 ACM Conference on Computer and Communications Security, pp. 217–228 (2012)
4. Bagheri, H., Kang, E., Malek, S., Jackson, D.: A formal approach for detection of security flaws in the Android permission system. Formal Aspects Comput. **30**(5), 525–544 (2017). https://doi.org/10.1007/s00165-017-0445-z
5. Bello-Ogunu, E., Shehab, M.: PERMITME: integrating Android permissioning support in the IDE. In: Proceedings of the 2014 Workshop on Eclipse Technology eXchange, pp. 15–20 (2014)
6. Betarte, G., Campo, J., Cristiá, M., Gorostiaga, F., Luna, C., Sanz, C.: Towards formal model-based analysis and testing of Android's security mechanisms. In: 2017 XLIII Latin American Computer Conference (CLEI), pp. 1–10. IEEE (2017)
7. Betarte, G., Campo, J., Luna, C., Romano, A.: Formal analysis of Android's permission-based security model. Sci. Ann. Comput. Sci. **26**(1), 27–68 (2016)
8. Betarte, G., Campo, J., Luna, C., Sanz, C., Gorostiaga, F., Cristiá, M.: A formal approach for the verification of the permission-based security model of Android. CLEI Electron. J. **21**(2) (2018)
9. Buchanan, W.: Introduction to Security and Network Forensics. Taylor & Francis (2011). https://books.google.fr/books?id=8uzM63AYi_MC
10. Chester, P., Jones, C., Mkaouer, M.W., Krutz, D.E.: M-Perm: a lightweight detector for Android permission gaps. In: 4th International Conference on Mobile Software Engineering and Systems (MOBILESoft), pp. 217–218. IEEE (2017)
11. Fang, Z., Han, W., Li, Y.: Permission based android security: issues and countermeasures. Comput. Secur. **43**, 205–218 (2014)
12. Fragkaki, Elli, Bauer, Lujo, Jia, Limin, Swasey, David: Modeling and enhancing Android's permission system. In: Foresti, Sara, Yung, Moti, Martinelli, Fabio (eds.) ESORICS 2012. LNCS, vol. 7459, pp. 1–18. Springer, Heidelberg (2012). https://doi.org/10.1007/978-3-642-33167-1_1
13. Guo, W.: Management system for secure mobile application development. In: Proceedings of the ACM Turing Celebration Conference, China, pp. 1–4 (2019)

14. He, X.: Modeling and analyzing the Android permission framework using high level Petri Nets. In: 2017 IEEE International Conference on Software Quality, Reliability and Security (QRS), pp. 232–239. IEEE (2017)

15. Hoffmann, J., Ussath, M., Holz, T., Spreitzenbarth, M.: Slicing droids: program slicing for smali code. In: Proceedings of the 28th Annual ACM Symposium on Applied Computing, pp. 1844–1851 (2013)

16. Jha, A.K., Lee, S., Lee, W.J.: Developer mistakes in writing Android manifests: an empirical study of configuration errors. In: 2017 IEEE/ACM 14th International Conference on Mining Software Repositories (MSR), pp. 25–36. IEEE (2017)

17. Saaltink, M.: The Z/EVES system. In: Bowen, J.P., Hinchey, M.G., Till, D. (eds.) ZUM 1997. LNCS, vol. 1212, pp. 72–85. Springer, Heidelberg (1997). https://doi.org/10.1007/BFb0027284

18. Sadeghi, A., Jabbarvand, R., Ghorbani, N., Bagheri, H., Malek, S.: A temporal permission analysis and enforcement framework for Android. In: Proceedings of the 40th International Conference on Software Engineering, ICSE 2018, pp. 846–857. ACM, New York (2018)

19. Scoccia, G.L., Peruma, A., Pujols, V., Malavolta, I., Krutz, D.E.: Permission issues in open-source Android apps: an exploratory study. In: 2019 19th International Working Conference on Source Code Analysis and Manipulation (SCAM), pp. 238–249. IEEE (2019)

20. Seo, J., Kim, D., Cho, D., Shin, I., Kim, T.: FLEXDROID: enforcing in-app privilege separation in Android. In: NDSS (2016)

21. Spivey, J.M.: Z Notation - A Reference Manual, 2nd edn. Prentice Hall International Series in Computer Science. Prentice Hall (1992)

22. Vidas, T., Christin, N., Cranor, L.: Curbing Android permission creep. In: Proceedings of the Web, vol. 2, pp. 91–96 (2011)

23. Wu, S., Liu, J.: Overprivileged permission detection for Android applications. In: ICC 2019–2019 IEEE International Conference on Communications (ICC), pp. 1–6. IEEE (2019)

24. Xu, G., Xu, S., Gao, C., Wang, B., Xu, G.: PerHelper: helping developers make better decisions on permission uses in Android apps. Appl. Sci. 9(18), 3699 (2019)

Design of a Trustworthy and Resilient Data Sharing Platform for Healthcare Provision

Matthew Banton[ID], Juliana Bowles[ID], Agastya Silvina[ID], and Thais Webber[✉][ID]

School of Computer Science, University of St Andrews, St Andrews KY16 9SX, UK
jkfb@st-andrews.ac.uk

Abstract. Healthcare data sharing platforms have been gaining prominence over the last decade, especially with the emergence of technologies dedicated to increase system security and users' privacy. Moreover, these platforms are becoming less centralised as time progresses, with need for more data from a variety of locations and settings to be transferred between authorised parties. These requirements also include legal and ethical concerns when creating such solution. Through data sharing, organisations can gain access to previously unknown information or higher quality data, share research findings, and make decisions based on larger (and hopefully more representative) datasets. Such platform should be resilient to attack or loss of data and be able to recover quickly and efficiently from unexpected events. This paper focuses on the blend of emerging technologies (data lake and blockchain) in a design to provide secure and resilient data sharing to only those patients and healthcare professionals authorised to access it across multiple European countries.

Keywords: Healthcare · Data sharing systems · Security · Resilience

1 Introduction

Healthcare provision has been the target of different technological advances over the decades, ranging from processes improvement within organisations to data and devices integration for real-time access [3,9,13]. Medical data sources have become less centralised with more data being used in a variety of settings and for different purposes. Several challenges arise from the distributed nature of medical data, including confidentiality issues such as how to securely and reliably share the data with different healthcare providers whilst preserving patients' privacy [9,13,20]. This has led to the inclusion of security and resilience aspects early in the development of such systems [7,13,14,19].

Currently, a focal point in the European healthcare domain is the development of flexible and secure data sharing platforms for healthcare provision

The research in this paper was supported by the EU H2020 project SERUMS: Securing Medical Data in Smart Patient-Centric Healthcare Systems (grant code 826278).

including emerging technologies [11,12,18]. This comes with a variety of legal, ethical and technical challenges such as protecting sensitive health information under different legislation [16] together with the ability to control and audit the access to the confidential medical data [12,14].

An important aspect when designing data sharing systems is organising the architectural key assets so that they can be protected at different layers against external events and malicious users that could cause, for instance, breaches in both data integrity and confidentiality; and to have strategies to resist, detect and to restore the system normal functioning after an outage occurs [22]. Resilience reflects the ability of a system to continue to deliver essential functions and services to legitimate users while it is under occurrence of unexpected events as well as refers to its ability to recover from those events [22]. Literature also defines resilience based on failure probabilities aiming to reduce the impact of disruptive situations by minimising the probability of failures in the first instance, and then reducing the consequences of disruptive events, thus improving system recovery time [10]. In data sharing systems design for healthcare, the approaches applied to ensure system resilience may contribute to the difference between life and death for patients, especially when professionals could have access to crucial health information provided by the system and the data is unavailable, missing or incorrect [13,17].

The EU Horizon 2020 research project Serums[1] [15,23] proposes an architectural model to share health information data, acquired from a variety of sources and formats, only to authorised individuals and healthcare organisations in a secure and efficient way. The ultimate platform goal is to be resilient to data corruption and breaches and allow a secure user-friendly access to only authorised users. Serums core design is a combination of data lake and blockchain technologies [6,23,24] that synergies to provide an indelible record of access requests and changes to data, while also allowing health centres to continue accessing their data as they see fit. Even with availability assured, it is critical that the system can be trusted to not disclose data to untrusted parties, and to not allow data breaches from unauthorised users, given the sensitive and confidential nature of medical data [21].

This paper aims to showcase the resilience characteristics on Serums platform design, and how these features can be beneficial to both withstand and recover from external unexpected events. Thus, we structure the paper as follows. Section 2 provide the details of the Serums architecture and how the various systems interlink and operate. Section 3 discusses the particular resilience aspects related to Serums' core technologies, blockchain and data lake, highlighting important security and performance aspects when introducing resilient properties in data sharing systems like Serums. Section 4 we conclude the paper summarising Serums platform design aspects towards achieving resilient characteristics.

---

[1] For more information refer to www.serums-h2020.org.

2   Data Sharing Platform Design

The Serums platform is a tool-chain [4,15] built to demonstrate the need for and the advantages of an integrated data sharing platform for healthcare provision in Europe, ensuring privacy to users and security when accessing medical records [2,8]. The architectural design workflow [23] describes the overall system design process and detail its core functionalities [5,6].

Figure 1 illustrates Serums platform components and their connections, as well as its potential end-users (individuals and organisations), and the expected interconnection with other external medical data sources. Serums Smart Health Centre System (SHCS) integrates essential technologies for building layered security attributes since design. The core layers to securely process users requests in the Serums platform are, respectively, the authentication component [8] (user login feature), the blockchain component [5] (user authorisation to access data and personalised access rules creation) and the data lake component [6] (fine-grained medical data retrieval).

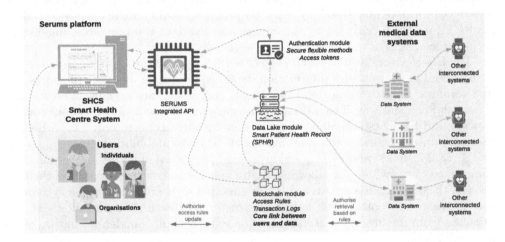

Fig. 1. Serums platform overview: core components, users and interactions

Authentication is the first layer of security in the system. Serums proposes new flexible techniques to the user create passwords and authenticate themselves in such a way it is less likely the occurrence of security breaches [2,8]. This component acts as a certifying agent for the authenticity of users and confirms to other modules that they can meet the requests originated from these users.

A core module in Serums architecture is the Blockchain component, which is the core link between individuals and medical data, since it authorises the users to access medical records and other data sharing features within the platform like personalised access rules creation. This component stores the access rules as customised transparent fine-grained access permissions to individuals, and it is responsible for keeping immutable logs of all requested transactions.

Access rules formally are defined as strict tuples identifying the 'who' (patient), 'to whom' (professionals), 'what' (parts of medical data) and 'when' (validity of the rule) the data can be shared in the platform front-end after successful authentication into the system. These rules state always up-to-date information on access privileges and provide on-demand check for retrieval eligibility [5]. Exploiting blockchain technology in this way allows for greater resilience than a standard database with access lists [12], as the indelible nature of the blockchain ensures that all transactions are logged, and the distributed aspect ensures that there is not a single entity that has control over the access rules. For more detail on the blockchain component setup and behaviour, as well as access rules creation formal approach please refer to [5,6].

Finally, the data lake component manages the medical data, as well as provides an area for medical centres to securely upload that data for processing. Tags (or labels) are added to the data by their providers, to define the data purpose and subsequent retrieval granularity [6]. This feature, when combined with filters and rules within the platform, ensures that the authorised users allowed to access only a subset of a patient data, only retrieve that specific subset of data from the medical centres systems [5]. Storing only metadata and access rules on-chain, using a data lake to manage the data, like Serums does, integrating records in unified way (SPHR - Smart Patient Health Record [6]), allows the scale of the data sharing platform as the European medical healthcare provision system requires [6,9,15].

It is worth mentioning that all of Serums core technologies have weaknesses that have been mentioned in previous literature [1,11,24]. However, Serums attempts to account for these vulnerabilities by employing an holistic system, which allows the components strengths to synergise with one another [2,23].

3   Blockchain and Data Lake Components Resilience

This section describes how Serums can potentially reduce the occurrence of disruptive events and how it would react when they occur. Following, we highlight the characteristics that increase Serums platform's ability to minimise the impacts of these events and restore its normal operation afterwards.

- **Potential resilience of a distributed database:** Blockchain as a distributed database can allow alternative nodes to take over if one goes down. The advantage of using blockchain in the way Serums platform does is that it ensures availability of the rules to control the access over medical data through the Serums Data Lake. If the local node were to go down, or even the data lake component of the system, then patients could still update rules relating to their data. These rules would then be updated on the local node when it is returned to service. Another important aspect is medical centres are integrated within Serums, each one has its own node on the blockchain, with each node replicating the other nodes. They decide individually on what the data should be, and through consensus it increases the probability that data is correct, with each medical centre contributing to the whole chain, there is no single entity controlling the data.

- **Advantages of immutability with regards to resilience:** sharing the access rules in the way Serums does, makes tampering a difficult task [2]. A malicious user would need to find a way to gain access to accounts that have legitimate access to change the required rules (e.g., phishing), rather than use injection type attacks to alter the state of rules. Even in the case of an attacker being able to gain access to a legitimate account and alter rules, the scope will be limited by the access to medical records of that account [2]. Logs will be recorded onto the chain containing the transaction undertaken, the grantor and grantee, as well as the date and time of its occurrence. The indelible nature of the blockchain means that these logs are correct, and free from any malicious influence (something malicious actors do when they seek to infiltrate a system covertly). In case the access rules are overwritten by users, it is a trivial task to track the origin of these changes by analysing the immutable blockchain logs and return the rules in place to their previous state. Activity logs captured by the blockchain component are essential assets for determining suspicious or failed transactions. They provide useful information for defining the actions to reduce the impact of disruptive events as how to safely restore system to a reliable state of operation.
- **Only essential data storage in the blockchain:** the medical data is not on-chain itself in Serums. The reason is that when data that must be stored on-chain is larger than the blocks, it can impact performance negatively, leading to system disruption and "brown-outs" (i.e., restriction on the availability of particular features). Data lakes, however, are perfectly suited for big data applications and storing large volumes of data. As such, to increase resilience we use both a data lake to store medical data, and the blockchain to manage access and log requests.
- **Coordinated data processing on the data lake:** a common issue for data lakes is becoming a dumping ground for data, and transforming into a "data swamp" [11]. This naturally affects the availability of data, as if useful data cannot be found, then it might as well not be there. Serums combats this particular issue through using a four-stage process:
  - Stage 1: the authorised medical data is selected from data sources according to authorised tags and uploaded to the raw zone of the data lake.
  - Stage 2: structure is added to the medical data, through the use of scripts. The data itself will stay in the raw zone, however the metadata added to it (SPHR) will be added to a structured zone, which allows the data to become efficiently searchable.
  - Stage 3: this stage deals with SPHR access specifically. Relevant data is searched from the structured zone and uploaded from the unstructured zone to the curated zone. This zone is encrypted to ensure integrity. After the health record is sent, the contents of the curated zone are deleted.
  - Stage 4: finally, the completed SPHR is moved to the consumer zone, where it can be accessed. Again, this is a temporary zone, and is encrypted

to ensure integrity. The consumer zone is the only zone where completed SPHR can be accessed from.

Focusing on resilience, we highlight that the data lake also holds two other areas that extract data from the structured (and unstructured) areas: the Workspace and Analytics zones. These zones are for developers to work without risk of any data being destroyed.

- **Extensive use of metadata:** The data lake metadata is used extensively, and actual medical data are accessed only sparingly when absolutely required by authorised users. This allows for greater availability of data on the platform, as the metadata of a medical record can be updated in nearly real-time. For example, if a file is missing from the unstructured zone, the metadata will allow the system to determine where the data came from, and re-upload a copy for use. Additionally, medical centres' own systems will not rely on Serums platform being online, but they could potentially benefit from having an additional copy of the data available from Serums (e.g., for backup purposes) as long as it respects the data protection legislation and recommended standards [16].

4   Conclusion

We have discussed how Serums attempts to ensure that the platform is resilient to data breaches, leaks, or even corruption, and how parts of the Serums system could go down without impacting other areas. However, these features, while aiding resilience overall, would not ensure a resilient system themselves. Typical backups would still be required, as well as well-defined processes to determine how and when to initiate and use those backup procedures.

A contributing factor to Serums resilience, is that it only manages copies of medical data, meaning that should the Serums system go down, local medical records and systems are not affected. This means that should Serums go down, local systems and processes can continue as normal, and then changes and updates be uploaded once Serums comes back online. When combined with the modular engineering approach, which means that aspects of Serums could fail without impacting other areas, we believe this could result in a system that is unlikely to suffer large scale failures and be more easily recovered in case of system disruption.

There are effectively only two components that could stop most of the Serums functionalities should they fail. The first component is the web portal, which would logically block users from accessing the system if it were to go down. However, even this would not cause all functionalities to be unavailable, as data is uploaded to the data lake, and any analysis can be performed independently of the web portal as a measure to increase resilience. The second component is the blockchain, which is essential for authorising users' access to medical data, and if it were to fail then users would therefore not be able to gain the permissions necessary to access the data. It can be argued that the blockchain is the most resilient aspect of the system, however, it being distributed between multiple medical centres. If one medical centre version were to go offline, then users would be directed to another node. The nodes are not user-centric, and all store a copy of each other's data. When the offline node comes back online, it can copy any changes made while it was offline. In the meantime, the worst scenario is that access is delayed slightly due to larger hops to ensure access permissions.

The different technologies involved in Serums also have different trade-offs, but their advantages can function together to build a holistic system that is resistant to errors or failures. For instance, disadvantages of the blockchain when it comes to big data are mitigated by the data lake, while its advantages include immutable logs and records of system access and respective transactions, which can aid in system recovery.

The Serums platform allows the components to communicate and effectively operate together, depending on functionality required, with no tighter integration that could cause a cascading failure in the event of one component failing. We believe the blend of these technologies brings key attributes to enable a secure and resilient data sharing platform for healthcare provision, combining blockchain to log any activity and allow easy restoration, with a data lake which is perfectly suited to this kind of large-scale data platform.

Acknowledgment. We thank all our partners and universities who contribute to the Serums project design and development.

References

1. Abu-elezz, I., Hassan, A., Nazeemudeen, A., Househ, M., Abd-alrazaq, A.: The benefits and threats of blockchain technology in healthcare: a scoping review. Int. J. Med. Inform. **142**, 104246 (2020)
2. Banton, M., Bowles, J., Silvina, A., Webber, T.: On the benefits and security risks of a user-centric data sharing platform for healthcare provision. In: UMAP 2021 Adjunct: Publication of the 29th ACM Conference on User Modeling, Adaptation and Personalization, pp. 351–356. ACM, New York (2021)
3. Bardhan, I.R., Thouin, M.F.: Health information technology and its impact on the quality and cost of healthcare delivery. Decis. Support Syst. **55**(2), 438–449 (2013)
4. Bowles, J., Mendoza-Santana, J., Webber, T.: Interacting with next-generation smart patient-centric healthcare systems. In: UMAP 2020 Adjunct: Publication of the 28th ACM Conf. on User Modeling, Adaptation and Personalization, pp. 192–193. ACM, New York (2020)
5. Bowles, J., Webber, T., Blackledge, E., Vermeulen, A.: A blockchain-based healthcare platform for secure personalised data sharing. Stud. Health Technol. Inform. Public Health Inform. **281**, 208–212 (2021)
6. Bowles, J.K.F., Mendoza-Santana, J., Vermeulen, A.F., Webber, T., Blackledge, E.: Integrating healthcare data for enhanced citizen-centred care and analytics. Stud. Health Technol. Inform. **275**, 17–21 (2020)
7. Chen, J., Lv, Z., Song, H.: Design of personnel big data management system based on blockchain. Future Gener. Comput. Syst. **101**, 1122–1129 (2019)

8. Constantinides, A., Belk, M., Fidas, C., Pitsillides, A.: Design and development of the serums patient-centric user authentication system. In: UMAP 2020 Adjunct: Publication of the 28th ACM Conference on User Modeling, Adaptation and Personalization, pp. 201–203. ACM, New York, July 2020

9. Dhayne, H., Haque, R., Kilany, R., Taher, Y.: In search of big medical data integration solutions - a comprehensive survey. IEEE Access **7**, 91265–91290 (2019)

10. Dinh, L.T., Pasman, H., Gao, X., Mannan, M.S.: Resilience engineering of industrial processes: Principles and contributing factors. J. Loss Prev. Process Ind. **25**(2), 233–241 (2012)

11. Gavrilov, G., Vlahu-Gjorgievska, E., Trajkovik, V.: Healthcare data warehouse system supporting cross-border interoperability. Health Inform. J. **26**(2), 1321–1332 (2020)

12. Guo, H., Li, W., Nejad, M., Shen, C.C.: Access control for electronic health records with hybrid blockchain-edge architecture. In: Access Control for Electronic Health Records with Hybrid Blockchain-edge Architecture, pp. 44–51. IEEE (2019)

13. Hathaliya, J.J., Tanwar, S.: An exhaustive survey on security and privacy issues in healthcare 4.0. Comput. Commun. **153**, 311–335 (2020)

14. Hölbl, M., Kompara, M., Kamišalić, A., Nemec Zlatolas, L.: A systematic review of the use of blockchain in healthcare. Symmetry **10**(10), 470 (2018)

15. Janjic, V., Bowles, J., et al.: The serums tool-chain: Ensuring security and privacy of medical data in smart patient-centric healthcare systems. In: 2019 IEEE International Conference on Big Data, pp. 2726–2735. IEEE, New York (2019)

16. Larrucea, X., Moffie, M., Asaf, S., Santamaria, I.: Towards a GDPR compliant way to secure European cross border healthcare industry 4.0. Comput. Stand. Interf. **69**, 103408 (2020)

17. Meingast, M., Roosta, T., Sastry, S.: Security and privacy issues with health care information technology. In: 2006 International Conference of the IEEE Engineering in Medicine and Biology Society, pp. 5453–5458. IEEE (2006)

18. Mettler, M.: Blockchain technology in healthcare: the revolution starts here. In: In: 2016 IEEE 18th International Conference on e-health Networking, Applications and Services (Healthcom), pp. 1–3. IEEE (2016)

19. Miyachi, K., Mackey, T.K.: hOCBS: a privacy-preserving blockchain framework for healthcare data leveraging an on-chain and off-chain system design. Inf. Process. Manage. **58**(3), 102535 (2021)

20. Rhahla, M., Allegue, S., Abdellatif, T.: Guidelines for GDPR compliance in big data systems. J. Inf. Secur. Appl. **61**, 102896 (2021)

21. Seh, A.H., et al.: Healthcare data breaches: insights and implications. Healthcare **8**(2), 133 (2020)

22. Trivedi, K.S., Kim, D.S., Ghosh, R.: Resilience in computer systems and networks. In: 2009 IEEE/ACM International Conference on Computer-Aided Design-Digest of Technical Papers, pp. 74–77. IEEE (2009)

23. Webber, T., Santana, J.M., Vermeulen, A.F., Bowles, J.K.F.: Designing a patient-centric system for secure exchanges of medical data. In: Gervasi, O., et al. (eds.) ICCSA 2020. LNCS, vol. 12254, pp. 598–614. Springer, Cham (2020). https://doi.org/10.1007/978-3-030-58817-5_44

24. Yue, X., Wang, H., Jin, D., Li, M., Jiang, W.: Healthcare data gateways: found healthcare intelligence on blockchain with novel privacy risk control. J. Med. Syst. **40**(10), 1–8 (2016)

Author Index

Printed in the United States
by Baker & Taylor Publisher Services

Printed in the United States
by Baker & Taylor Publisher Services